BY COMMAND OF His late Majesty WILLIAM THE IV.TH
and under the Patronage of
Her Majesty the Queen.

HISTORICAL RECORDS,

OF THE

British Army

Comprising the

History of every Regiment

IN HER MAJESTY'S SERVICE.

By Richard Cannon Esqr

Adjutant Generals Office, Horse Guards.

London.

Printed by Authority.

HISTORICAL RECORD

OF

THE THIRTEENTH, FIRST SOMERSET,

OR,

THE PRINCE ALBERT'S REGIMENT

OF

LIGHT INFANTRY;

CONTAINING

AN ACCOUNT OF THE FORMATION OF THE REGIMENT
IN 1685,

AND OF ITS SUBSEQUENT SERVICES
TO 1848.

COMPILED BY
RICHARD CANNON, Esq.
ADJUTANT-GENERAL'S OFFICE, HORSE GUARDS.

ILLUSTRATED WITH PLATES.

The Naval & Military Press

Published by

The Naval & Military Press Ltd
Unit 5 Riverside, Brambleside
Bellbrook Industrial Estate
Uckfield, East Sussex
TN22 1QQ England

Tel: +44 (0)1825 749494

www.naval-military-press.com
www.nmarchive.com

In reprinting in facsimile from the original, any imperfections are inevitably reproduced and the quality may fall short of modern type and cartographic standards.

THE THIRTEENTH,

THE FIRST SOMERSET REGIMENT OF FOOT,

OR

THE PRINCE ALBERT'S REGIMENT OF LIGHT INFANTRY,

Bears on its Regimental Colour

THE SPHINX, WITH THE WORD "EGYPT,"

In Commemoration of its Services in Egypt in 1801;

THE WORD "MARTINIQUE,"

In Commemoration of its Services at the Capture of that Island on the 24th February, 1809;

AND THE WORDS

"AVA,"—"AFFGHANISTAN,"—"GHUZNEE,"—"JELLALABAD,"

WITH THE MURAL CROWN,

AND

"CABOOL, 1842,"

In Commemoration of its Arduous and Meritorious Services in the Asiatic Territories from 1839 to 1842.

THIRTEENTH, PRINCE ALBERT'S REGIMENT OF LIGHT INFANTRY.

CONTENTS.

Year		Page
1685	Formation of the Regiment	1
——	Station and Establishment	—
——	Earl of Huntingdon, and other officers appointed to Commissions	2
——	Encamped on Hounslow Heath . . .	—
1686	Establishment of the Regiment . . .	—
——	Uniform of the Regiment	—
——	Marched into Yorkshire and Cumberland .	—
——	Removed to Chester	—
1687	List of Officers	3
1688	Declaration of the Regiment in favour of the Protestant Interest	4
——	Colonel F. Hastings appointed in the place of the Earl of Huntingdon	—
1689	Proceeded to Edinburgh	5
——	Engaged at Killicrankie	6
——	Embarked for Ireland	8
1690	Engaged at the Battle of the Boyne . .	9
——	Embarked for England	—
——	Re-embarked for Ireland	—
——	Engaged at Cork and Kinsale . . .	10
1691	Engaged at Drumaugh and Ballycleugh . .	11
——	Took possession of Drummaneer . . .	—

CONTENTS.

Year		Page
1691	Engaged at Lismore	11
——	Termination of hostilities in Ireland	—
——	Embarked for England	—
1692	Selected to form part of an Expedition against the French Coast	12
——	Proceeded to Ostend	—
——	Returned to England	—
1693	Detachment sent to Flanders to replace the casualties of the Army after the Battle of Landen.	—
1695	Colonel F. Hastings cashiered, and Colonel Sir John Jacob appointed to succeed him	13
1697	Termination of the War in Flanders and the Establishment reduced	—
1699	Proceeded to Ireland	—
1700	Hostile measures of King Louis XIV. of France	—
1701	Embarked from Cork for Flanders.	14
——	Landed at Helvoetsluys	—
——	Reviewed at Breda by King William III.	—
1702	Encamped at Rosendael	—
——	Colonel the Earl of Barrymore appointed by purchase to succeed Sir John Jacob	—
1702	Engaged in the siege of Kayserswerth	—
——	The Earl of Marlborough assumed the command of the Army in Flanders	—
——	Formed in brigade under Brigadier General Frederick Hamilton.	15
1702	Engaged in the siege and capture of Venloo	—
——	——————————— of Fort St. Michael	—
——	——————————— of Ruremonde	16
——	——————————— of Liege	—
——	Entered winter-quarters at Breda	17
1703	Engaged in the siege of Huy.	—
——	——————————— of Limburg	—

CONTENTS.

Year		Page
1703	Spanish Guelderland delivered from France	17
——	Embarked for England	—
——	Proceeded to Portugal.	—
1704	Encamped at Estremos.	18
——	Embarked for Gibraltar	19
1705	Engaged in defence of Gibraltar	20
——	Re-embarked for Spain	21
——	Engaged in the siege of Barcelona.	22
——	—— in storming Fort Montjuich	—
——	—— in relief of St. Matheo in Valencia	23
1706	Formed by the Earl of Peterborough into a Regiment of Cavalry commanded by Colonel Edward Pearce	24
——	Marched to Oropeso and formed into eight troops	25
——	Remainder of the Regiment sent to England to recruit.	—
——	Pearce's Regiment of Dragoons engaged in Valencia	26
1707	———————————— at Almanza	—
1708	Thirteenth Regiment, having been recruited, again embarked for Portugal, and encamped between Elvas and Campo Mayor	27
1709	Proceeded to the banks of the Caya	—
——	Engaged at the attack on the Caya	—
——	Colonel the Earl of Barrymore taken prisoner.	28
1710	Served the Campaign on the frontiers of Portugal	—
1711	Embarked from Portugal for Gibraltar.	—
1713	Received volunteers from several Corps disbanded after the peace of Utrecht.	—
1715	Colonel the Earl of Barrymore succeeded by Colonel Stanhope Cotton, then Lieutenant-Governor of Gibraltar	29
1725	Colonel Cotton died, and succeeded as Colonel of the Thirteenth Regiment by Lord Mark Kerr	—

CONTENTS.

Year		Page
1727	Engaged in a second successful defence of Gibraltar against the Spaniards	29
1728	Relieved from duty at Gibraltar, after foreign service for twenty years	30
1730	Reviewed on Winkfield-plain, with the Twelfth foot, by King George II.	—
1732	Colonel Lord Mark Kerr removed to the Eleventh Dragoons, and succeeded by Colonel John Middleton	—
1739	Colonel John Middleton died, and succeeded by Colonel Henry Pulteney	—
——	War declared against Spain, and augmentation took place	—
1740	Encamped on Windsor Forest	—
1741	Encamped on Lexden Heath	31
1742	Embarked for Flanders under the Earl of Stair	—
1743	War declared against France	—
——	Encamped at Aschaffenburg	—
——	Engaged at the battle of Dettingen	—
1744	Engaged under Field Marshal Wade on the banks of the Scheldt	32
1745	Engaged at the battle of Fontenoy	—
——	Encamped on the plains of Lessines	33
——	Arrival of Charles Edward, elder son of the Pretender, in Scotland	—
——	Thirteenth Regiment returned from Flanders, and landed at Blackwall	34
——	Proceeded to Doncaster and Newcastle	—
1746	Engaged at Falkirk-moor	--
——	———— at Culloden-moor	35
——	Rebellion in Scotland suppressed	36
——	Flight of the Young Pretender	—
——	Regiment returned to Holland	—

CONTENTS.

Year		Page
1746	Advanced to Maestricht, and thence to Liege .	36
—	Engaged at Roucoux	—
1747	Engaged at Val	37
1748	Employed in Limburg, and in North Brabant .	39
—	Treaty of Peace at Aix la Chapelle . .	—
—	Returned to England	—
·1751	Royal Warrant issued regulating the clothing, and colours of Regiments	—
1754	Embarked for Gibraltar	—
1762	Returned to England	—
1766	His Royal Highness the Duke of Gloucester appointed Colonel in succession to Honorable Henry Pulteney	40
1767	Reviewed in Hyde Park with the Twelfth Foot, by King George III.	—
—	The Duke of Gloucester appointed to the Third Foot Guards, and succeeded in the Colonelcy by Honorable James Murray . . .	—
1768	Proceeded to Ireland	—
1769	Embarked for Minorca	—
1776	Returned to England	—
1781	Embarked for the West Indies . . .	41
1782	The war with America ceased and the regiment returned to England	—
—	The Regiment directed to assume the County title of First Somersetshire Regiment . .	—
1784	Embarked for Ireland	—
1789	General George Ainslie appointed Colonel in succession to Honorable James Murray .	—
1790	Embarked for Jamaica	42
1793	Embarked for St. Domingo	—
1794	Proceeded on an expedition under Colonel John Whitaker to Cape Tiburon . . .	43
—	Engaged at the Post of L'Acal . . .	44

CONTENTS.

Year		Page
1794	Engaged at Port au-Prince	44
	——— at Fort Bizzeton	45
1796	Re-embarked for England	—
1797	Proceeded to Ireland	—
1800	Embarked for England	46
	Embarked on an expedition to the Coast of Spain	—
	Proceeded to Gibraltar and Malta . . .	47
1801	Joined the expedition to Egypt under General Sir Ralph Abercromby	—
	Landed at Aboukir	48
	Advanced to Alexandria, and engaged the French on 12th March	—
	Engaged a second time at Alexandria against " Buonaparte's Invincibles" on the 21st of March	49
	French Army expelled from Egypt . .	—
	The Grand Seignior conferred orders of Knighthood and Gold Medals on the Officers. .	50
	Authorized to bear the " Sphinx," and the word " Egypt" on the Colours and Appointments.	—
1802	Embarked from Egypt for Malta . . .	51
1803	Embarked for Gibraltar	—
1804	General Ainslie died, and Lieut. General A. Campbell appointed to the Colonelcy . .	—
	Epidemic fever prevailed at Gibraltar which occasioned many casualties . . .	52
1805	Embarked for England	—
1806	Proceeded from Portsmouth to Ramsgate .	—
1807	Embarked for Ireland	—
	Completed by Militia Volunteers, and re-embarked for England	—
1808	Embarked for the West Indies and proceeded to Bermuda	—

Year		Page
1808	Joined an expedition against Martinique.	53
1809	Stationed at Martinique	54
1810	Joined an expedition against Guadaloupe.	—
1811 1812	}Stationed at Martinique	—
1813	Lieut.-General Edward Morrison appointed to the Colonelcy in succession to General Campbell, removed to the thirty-second regiment .	—
——	Embarked from Martinique for Canada . .	55
——	Proceeded on an expedition to Plattsburg .	—
1814	Defended a post on the La Cole river against a numerous Corps of Americans . . .	56
1815	Peace concluded with the United States of America	57
——	Embarked from Canada and landed at Portsmouth	58
——	Proceeded to Jersey	—
1817	Presentation of new Colours . . .	—
——	Proceeded to Guernsey	59
1819	Embarked for Portsmouth	60
——	——————— Scotland	61
1820	——————— Ireland	—
1822	——————— Liverpool	62
——	Proceeded to Edinburgh	—
——	Furnished Guards of Honour to King George IV. on his visit to Scotland	—
——	Proceeded to Chatham to prepare for embarkation for India	—
——	Constituted a regiment of Light Infantry .	—
1823	Embarked for Bengal	—
1824	Employed in the war with the King of Ava .	63
——	Capture of *Rangoon*, the principal city of the Burmese Empire	—
——	Detached against the Island of Cheduba .	—

xxxii   CONTENTS.

Year		Page
1824	Advanced against formidable stockades erected by the Burmese	64
——	Repeated attacks of the Burmese on the British possessions	65
——	Attack on the Burmese in the neighbourhood of Rangoon	66
——	Another victorious attack under Majors Dennie and Sale	67
——	Further attacks followed up	68
1825	Proceeded against the city of Bassein	69
——	Embarked for Rangoon	70
——	Proceeded to join the army at Prome	—
——	Advanced to attack the Burmese at Simbike	71
——	Again marched to attack the enemy at Napadee Hills	—
1826	Advanced and took post at Melloon	72
——	Engaged with the Burmese at Pagahm Mew	73
——	Advanced upon the capital, Ummerapoora	—
——	Treaty of peace concluded with the King of Ava	—
——	Order of thanks from the Governor-General of India for services performed in this arduous campaign	74
——	Authorized to bear the word "Ava" on its colours and appointments	—
——	Embarked for Calcutta	—
——	—————— Berhampore	—
1827	Arrived at Dinapore	—
1831	Proceeded to Agra	—
1836	Marched to Kurnaul	—
1837	A detachment proceeded to Lahore with the Commander-in-Chief on a visit to Runjeet Singh, the ruler of the Sikhs	75
——	Detachment returned to Kurnaul	—

CONTENTS.   xxxiii

Year		Page
1838	War with the chiefs of Affghanistan	76
——	Joined the army of the Indus, proceeded to Ferozepore, and encamped on the banks of the river Gharra.	—
——	Marched to Bhawulpore	77
1839	Arrived at Roree, and took possession of Bakkur	78
——	Crossed the river Indus and arrived at Shikarpore	—
——	Continued its march to Beloochistan	—
——	Penetrated the Bolan Pass	79
——	Marched through the Vale of Shawl	—
——	Arrived at Candahar	—
——	Advanced to Ghuznee	80
——	Stormed and captured the citadel of Ghuznee	81
——	Shah Shoojah-ool-Moolk restored to his dominions in Affghanistan	82
——	Rewards to the conquerors of Affghanistan	83
——	Remained in Affghanistan to support the government of the restored Shah	84
——	Encamped near Cabool	—
1840	Advanced against Dost Mahomed in the Kohistan of Cabool.	—
——	Assisted in carrying the town and forts of Tootumdurra	—
——	Engaged in the attack of Julgar	85
——	———————— of Babookooshghur	86
——	———————— at Purwan	—
——	Returned to Cabool	—
1841	War recommenced with the Affghans	—
——	Attempt of the Affghans to expel Shah Shoojah	—
——	Marched to the Khoord Cabool Pass	—
——	———— Tezeen	87
——	———— Gundamuck	88
——	Engaged at the Jugdulluck Pass	—

xxxiv   CONTENTS.

Year		Page
1841	Captured the Fort of Mamoo Khail	88
——	Returned to Gundamuck	—
——	Captured the town of Jellalabad	89
1842	Defended the town	—
——	Defeated the Affghans	—
——	Renewed attempts of the Affghans to expel the British from the Cabool territory	90
——	Means adopted for a general attack on the Affghan camp	91
——	Death of Colonel Dennie	92
——	Defeat of Mahomed Akbar	93
——	Expression of approbation and thanks by the Governor-General of the conduct of Major-General Sir Robert Sale, and of the army under his command	94
——	—————————— of the houses of Parliament to the army in Affghanistan	95
——	Arrival at Jellalabad of the forces under Major-General Pollock	97
——	Major-General Sir Robert Sale's report of the services and privations of the troops for five months	98
——	Her Majesty's approbation and marks of distinction conferred on the Thirteenth regiment	101
——	Marched from Jellalabad to Gundamuck	102
——	The Affghans defeated at Jugdulluck	103
——	Actions at Tezeen, and in the Huft Kotul Pass	104
——	Re-occcupied Cabool	—
——	Detachment marched to meet the prisoners detained by Akbar Khan on their release and return to Cabool	—
——	Quitted the Affghan territory on return to India	105
——	Marched to Jellalabad	—
——	Proceeded to Peshawur	—

CONTENTS. XXXV

Year.		Page
1842	Proceeded across the Punjaub to Ferozepore	105
——	Received with military honours by the troops at the several stations on the route to India, by orders of the Governor-General	—
——	Received the Queen's authority to bear "CABOOL, 1842" on the colours and appointments	106
1843	Marched from Ferozepore to Mowbarukpore	107
——	Proceeded to Kussowlie	—
——	Marched to Ferozepore	—
——	Embarked for Sukkur	—
——	Major-General Sir Robert Sale appointed to the colonelcy of the Thirteenth regiment, in succession to General Morrison, deceased	—
1844	Moved to Kurrachee	108
——	Embarked for Bombay	—
1845	Embarked for England	109
——	Arrived at Gravesend	—
——	Proceeded to Walmer	—
1846	Lieutenant-General Sir William M. Gomm appointed to the colonelcy in succession to Major-General Sir Robert Sale, killed at the battle of Moodkee, on the 18th December, 1845	—
——	Marched to Portsmouth	—
——	Presentation of new colours by Field Marshal His Royal Highness the Prince Albert	—
1847	Embarked for Ireland	112
——	The Conclusion	113
	Description of the Flags captured from the Affghans in the Year 1842	115

xxxvi   CONTENTS.

SUCCESSION OF COLONELS.

Year		Page
1685	Theophilus Earl of Huntingdon	117
1688	Ferdinand Hastings	118
1689	Sir John Jacob, Bart.	—
1702	James Earl of Barrymore	119
1715	Stanhope Cotton.	—
1725	Lord Mark Kerr	120
1732	Lord Middleton	121
1739	Henry Pulteney	—
1766	William Henry Duke of Gloucester	122
1767	Hon. James Murray	123
1789	George Ainslie	—
1804	Alexander Campbell	124
1813	Edward Morrison	125
1843	Robert Henry Sale	126
1846	William Maynard Gomm	128

PLATES.

		Page.
Colours of the Regiment	to face	1
Costume of the Regiment	,,	62
Standards captured from the Affghans in the Action at Jellalabad on the 7th April, 1842	,,	116

THIRTEENTH,
PRINCE ALBERT'S REGIMENT OF LIGHT INFANTRY.

QUEEN'S COLOR.

REGIMENTAL COLOR.

FOR CANNON'S MILITARY RECORDS.

HISTORICAL RECORD

OF

THE THIRTEENTH,

FIRST SOMERSETSHIRE REGIMENT;

OR

PRINCE ALBERT'S REGIMENT OF LIGHT INFANTRY.

WHEN JAMES DUKE OF MONMOUTH denounced the 1685
character and pretensions of King James II., asserted
his own claims to the throne, and organized a military
force to establish his authority, the small regular army
then in England was not deemed sufficiently numerous
for the protection of the crown and kingdom against
lawless usurpation, and a number of additional corps
of cavalry and infantry were embodied. Among the
noblemen who stood forward in support of the throne
at this important juncture, was THEOPHILUS, EARL OF
HUNTINGDON, who was appointed colonel of one of the
regiments ordered to be raised,—now THIRTEENTH
LIGHT INFANTRY,—by commission dated the 20th of
June, 1685.

This regiment was raised in the southern counties of
England, and its general rendezvous was at Buckingham, where the Earl of Huntingdon established his
head-quarters; it consisted of ten companies, which
were raised by Colonel the Earl of Huntingdon, Lieut-
Colonel Francis Villiers, Major Charles Morgan,

B

1685 Captains Watson Dixey, Thomas Condon, Thomas Skipworth,— Hildibran, John Tidcomb, Bryan Turner, and Charles Hatton; and a number of loyal men coming readily forward to enrol themselves under the colours of the regiment, it was speedily formed and quartered at Buckingham and Aylesbury. In the middle of July it was employed to guard prisoners taken after the overthrow of the rebel army at Sedgemoor.

The rebellion being suppressed, and the Duke of Monmouth beheaded, the King assembled many of the newly-raised corps on Hounslow Heath, where the Earl of Huntingdon's regiment encamped in the beginning of August: it was reviewed on the Heath by His Majesty; the officers and soldiers received the expression of the King's royal approbation of the ready manner in which they had come forward to support the throne at the hour of danger, and they afterwards marched into garrison at Hull.

On the 6th of January, 1686, the establishment was fixed at the following numbers and rates of pay, viz. (*see* p. 3).

1686 The uniform of the regiment was, round hats with broad brims, the brim turned up on one side, and ornamented with yellow ribands; scarlet coats lined with yellow; yellow breeches, and gray stockings; the pikemen were distinguished by white sashes tied round their waists.

In June the regiment was again encamped on Hounslow Heath, and in August it marched into Yorkshire and Cumberland; the head-quarters being at York, where it passed the winter.

From York the head-quarters were removed, in February, 1687, to Chester, where they remained during the following twelve months.

REGIMENT OF LIGHT INFANTRY.

1686

The Earl of Huntingdon's Regiment.	Pay per Day.		
STAFF.	£.	s.	d.
The Colonel, *as Colonel*	0	12	0
Lieut.-Colonel, *as Lieut.-Colonel*	0	7	0
Major, *as Major*	0	5	0
Chaplain	0	6	8
Chirurgeon 4s. and Mate 2s. 6d.	0	6	6
Adjutant	0	4	0
Quarter-Master and Marshal	0	4	0
Total Staff	2	5	2
THE COLONEL'S COMPANY.			
The Colonel, as Captain	0	8	0
Lieutenant	0	4	0
Ensign	0	3	0
Two Serjeants, 1s. 6d. each	0	3	0
Three Corporals, 1s. each	0	3	0
One Drummer	0	1	0
Fifty Soldiers, 8d. each	1	13	4
Total for one Company	2	15	4
Nine Companies more at the same rate	24	18	0
Total per day Per Annum £10,922 12s. 6d.	29	18	6

LIST OF OFFICERS IN 1687.

1687

Captains.	Lieutenants.	Ensigns.
Earl of Huntingdon, (col).	Thomas Carleton.	William Delavale.
	William Rhodesley.	Ralph Cudworth.
Ferdinando Hastings (lieut.-colonel)	John Hook.	Deacon Garrett.
	John Fry.	Henry Fern.
Robert Ingram (major)	John Sheldon.	John Orefeur.
Watson Dixie.	Talbot Lacells.	Ambrose Jones.
John Tidcomb.	George Comly.	Hussey Hastings.
Owen Macarty.	Michael Dunkin.	Joseph Byerley
Charles Hutton.	George Keyworth.	Thomas Knivetton.
Sir John Jacob.	Henry Walrond.	William Callow.
Thomas Condon.		
Charnock Heron.		

Christopher Viscount Hatton. } Bernard Ellis. William Hawley } { Company of grenadiers added to the regiment in 1687.

Gabriel Hastings, *Chaplain* Talbot Lacells, *Adjutant.*
Claudius Gilbert, *Chirurgeon.* John Evans, *Quarter-Master.*

1688 The regiment left Chester in April, 1688, and in June it pitched its tents on Hounslow Heath. In the meantime, the proceedings of the King, to establish Papacy and arbitrary government, had filled the country with alarm, and many of the nobility and gentry had solicited the Prince of Orange to come to England with a Dutch army, to aid them in opposing the measures of the court. The Earl of Huntingdon continued, however, faithful to the interests of the King, and his regiment was ordered into garrison at Plymouth, together with the Earl of Bath's (now Tenth) regiment. When the Prince of Orange landed, the garrison of Plymouth was divided in its political views: the governor, the Earl of Bath, and Lieut.-Colonel Hastings, of the THIRTEENTH (cousin of the Earl of Huntingdon), were in the Protestant interest; the Earl of Huntingdon, who was present, and performing the duties of commanding officer, with Lieut.-Colonel Sir Charles Carney, of the Tenth, were devoted to the Roman Catholic interest; but nearly all the officers and soldiers had espoused the Protestant cause. The Earl of Bath, Lieut.-Colonel Hastings, and several other officers, arrested the Earl of Huntingdon, Captain Owen Macarty, Lieutenant Talbot Lacells, and Ensign Ambrose Jones, of the THIRTEENTH, who were Roman Catholics, and afterwards declared for the Prince of Orange, in which the two regiments in garrison concurred. When the fortress of Plymouth was established in the Protestant interest, the arrested officers were released.

The army refusing to fight in the cause of Papacy and arbitrary government, King James fled to France and the Prince of Orange promoted Lieut.-Colonel FERDINANDO HASTINGS to the colonelcy of the regiment, by commission, dated 1688.

The accession of the Prince and Princess of Orange 1689 to the throne having met with some opposition in Scotland, the regiment was ordered thither; and on arriving at *Edinburgh*, in the spring of 1689, it was employed in the blockade of the *castle*, which the Duke of Gordon held for King James; at the same time Viscount Dundee was arousing the clans to arms.

While the regiment was at Edinburgh, Major General Hugh Mackay, commanding-in-chief in Scotland, was watching the motions of Viscount Dundee, and he sent orders for Colonel Ramsay to join him with six hundred men of the Scots Brigade, in the Dutch service. The colonel commenced his march, but was intimidated by the menacing attitude of the Athol men, and returned to Perth; when a hundred men of Berkeley's (now Fourth) dragoons, a hundred of the Thirteenth foot, and two hundred of Leven's newly-raised regiment (now Twenty-fifth), were ordered to join him. Thus reinforced, the Colonel commenced his march through Athole and Badenoch for Inverness; and with the aid of this detachment, Major-General Mackay chased the clans, under Viscount Dundee, from the low country, and compelled them to take refuge in the wilds of Lochaber: the detachment of the Thirteenth foot was afterwards stationed at Inverness; and the regiment was relieved from the blockade of Edinburgh Castle by the surrender of that fortress on the 13th of June.

After forcing Viscount Dundee to take refuge in Lochaber, Major-General Mackay proceeded to Edinburgh, where he learned that the clans expected to be joined by a reinforcement from Ireland, and would probably soon descend from the hilly country; the major-general, therefore, assembled the Thirteenth

1689 foot, and several other corps, and marched from Edinburgh, to watch the motions of the insurgent Highlanders. Arriving at Dunkeld, he received an express from Lord Murray, son of the Marquis of Athol, stating that part of Viscount Dundee's army had arrived at Blair; and in consequence of this information, he commenced his march at daybreak on the morning of Saturday, the 27th of July, towards the pass of Killicrankie,* to confront his opponents, and on this occasion the THIRTEENTH foot, commanded by their colonel, Ferdinando Hastings, formed the rear-guard, to cover the march of twelve hundred pack-horses, which carried the baggage of the army.

Entering the pass of Killicrankie, the troops moved along the east bank of the river Garry, by a narrow road, confined between a range of craggy precipices on one hand, and on the other the river, considerably below the road, rushing from rock to rock with a murmuring sound; and as the THIRTEENTH regiment emerged from this difficult defile with the baggage, the royal army was seen in order of battle, on some rising ground at the foot of a hill, on the summit of which appeared the insurgent host, under Viscount Dundee. The THIRTEENTH foot formed on the right of the line, the

* List of troops under Major-General Mackay, at the battle of *Killicrankie*, 27th July, 1689:—

CAVALRY.

Annandale's troop of horse } Afterwards incorporated in a regiment, now
Belhaven's   ,, ,, } the Seventh Hussars.

INFANTRY.

HASTINGS' Foot, now THIRTEENTH.
Leven's Foot, now Twenty-fifth.
Kenmare's Foot, afterwards disbanded.

Mackay's } *Scots' Brigade* in the Dutch Service, afterwards *Ninety-*
Balfour's } *fourth Regiment* in the British line; disbanded in Decem-
Ramsay's } ber, 1818.

One hundred of Hastings' and two hundred of Leven's, were detached at Inverness, and were consequently not at the battle of Killicrankie.

grenadier company on the flank, with a supply of 1689 hand-grenades, the musketeers formed two wings; and the pikemen stood in column in the centre. During two tedious hours of a bright summer evening the armies stood looking at each other; and about half an hour before sunset, the Highlanders moved slowly down the hill, barefooted, and stripped to their shirts, to commence the battle: as they descended, they quickened their pace, uttered a loud shout, and commenced an irregular fire of musketry, which produced little effect. The King's troops reserved their fire until the clans came within a few paces, and then by a regular discharge, with a sure aim, produced great havoc on the thick masses opposed to them; but at that moment the Highlanders threw down their muskets, drew their swords, and closed upon their opponents, who had not time to fix their bayonets in the muzzles of their muskets,* and being thus attacked, under peculiar disadvantages, many of the king's troops gave way.

The THIRTEENTH foot, commanded by Colonel Hastings, stood their ground with great gallantry, and the Highlanders were unable to make any impression on this brave regiment. After being repulsed in their attack on its front, the Highlanders attempted to turn its right flank, when Colonel Hastings wheeled his pikemen to the right, and by a determined charge routed the clans at that point. As the conquering pikemen of the THIRTEENTH were returning to their post in the centre of the regiment, they discovered that the other corps of the royal army were overpowered, and the soldiers flying in every direction; at the same time the Highlanders had discontinued the pursuit, to plunder

---

* The bayonet, at this period, was fixed by forcing the handle into the muzzle of the musket; the troops, therefore, could not fire with fixed bayonets.

1689 the baggage. At that moment Major-General Mackay galloped to the regiment; he collected the fragments of other corps to it, and retreated. In his memoirs of this war, published in 1833, Major-General Mackay commends the conduct of this regiment;* and in his life, published in 1836, the author (John Mackay, Esq., of Rockfield) states, 'HASTINGS, on the right, sus-'tained the reputation of the English lion, but all to 'no purpose, so far had the panic extended.' Yet it was to great purpose, for one corps was preserved entire, which enabled the commander-in-chief to make good his retreat to Stirling.

Viscount Dundee was killed in the action; and the loss of the clans, in killed and wounded, was much greater than that of the king's troops. Major-General Mackay called to his aid additional corps, resumed the offensive, and by a series of active and skilful operations, restricted the movements of the Highlanders so much, that they separated to their homes.

In the meantime King James had arrived in Ireland with a body of French troops, and all the country, excepting Inniskilling and Londonderry, was subjected to his dominion. To rescue Ireland from his power, an army was sent to that country, under the veteran Marshal Duke Schomberg, and the THIRTEENTH foot were ordered to take part in this enterprise.

* 'There was no regiment or troop with me but behaved like the vilest 'cowards in nature, except HASTINGS' (THIRTEENTH), and Lord Leven's '(Twenty-fifth), whom I most praise at such a degree, as I cannot but 'blame others.'—*Mackay's Despatch to the Duke of Hamilton.*

'I could learn of no commanding officer that misbehaved, though I con-'fess that my Lord Leven, Colonel HASTINGS, and their officers have dis-'tinguished themselves in this occasion above all others.'—*Mackay's Official Narrative of the Battle.*

'My Lord,—Your son has behaved himself with all his officers and 'soldiers extraordinarily well, as did also Colonel HASTINGS with his.'— *Mackay's letter to Lord Melville.*

The regiment embarked from Scotland in the begin- 1689
ning of October, landed at Carlingford on the 9th of
that month, and received orders to join the army encamped at Dundalk; but these orders were countermanded, and the regiment marched into quarters at
Armagh and Clownish, where it was stationed during
the winter.

In April, 1690, the THIRTEENTH were stationed 1690
at Belfast, and they had the gratification of serving in
the campaign of that year, under King William III.,
who commanded his army in Ireland in person. They
had the honour to contribute towards the gaining of
the battle of the *Boyne*, on the 1st of July, when the
army of King William forced the passage of the river
Boyne, overthrew the French and Irish forces under
King James, and gained a decisive victory.

After this victory, the regiment advanced with the
army towards Dublin, and it was stationed several weeks
in garrison in that city, under Brigadier-General
Trelawny.

In the meantime, considerable alarm had been produced in England by the defeat of the combined
English and Dutch fleets, under Admirals Lord Tor-
rington and Evertsen, by the French navy, under the
Count de Tourville. After this disaster, England was
menaced with invasion, and a body of French troops
landed on the western coast, and destroyed a village;
when the THIRTEENTH, and several other corps, were
ordered to return to England.

After landing at Portsmouth, the regiment was
encamped, for several weeks, near that fortress; and
when the alarm of invasion had passed away, it was
ordered to join the expedition against *Cork* and *Kinsale*,
under Lieut.-General the Earl of Marlborough, (after-

1690 wards the celebrated Duke of Marlborough). It embarked on this service in the middle of September, arrived in Cork roads on the 21st of that month, and the co-operation of part of the army on shore having been secured, the troops landed on the 23rd, and besieged the city of Cork. A breach having been made, the THIRTEENTH regiment was selected to form part of the storming party, which advanced to assault the town on the 28th of September; but before the soldiers gained the breach, the enemy hung out a white flag, and agreed to surrender.

The troops marched out of Cork on the 1st of October, arrived before *Kinsale* on the following day, and commenced the siege of the two forts. The old fort was taken by storm immediately, and the new fort surrendered on the 15th of October.

After taking part in these services, the regiment was stationed in garrison at Cork. The health of the men suffered from having been employed in sieges during inclement weather, and in the official returns the regiment is stated to have had 462 rank and file fit for duty, and 216 sick.

1691 In the spring of 1691, when the army took the field under General de Ginkell (afterwards Earl of Athlone), the THIRTEENTH were left in garrison at Cork, from whence they frequently sent out detachments in quest of the bands of Roman Catholic peasantry who prowled about the country in arms, committing every description of depredation. On one of these occasions, when Colonel Hastings was out with two hundred men of the regiment, and five hundred militia, he was informed that a party of the royal dragoons was surrounded by a numerous body of the enemy at *Drumaugh*, and he instantly marched to their relief. On arriving at the vicinity of *Ballycleugh*, he found the hedges on both sides of the road lined with opponents; when the soldiers of the Thirteenth rushed into the inclosures, killed fifty adversaries, and chased the remainder some distance. On the following morning the soldiers of the Thirteenth drove the Irish from Drumaugh, and liberated the party of the royal dragoons at that place.

1691

Soon after this exploit, Colonel Hastings marched out of Cork with a party of the regiment and some militia, and seized upon *Drummaneer*, an important post near the Blackwater.

On the 12th of September, Captain John Orefeur left Cork, with a detachment of the regiment, to scour the country; and arriving in the vicinity of *Lismore*, he encountered a numerous body of armed partisans of King James, whom he instantly attacked, killed twenty of their number upon the spot, and put the remainder to flight, which so alarmed the armed bands of Roman Catholic peasantry, that they did not again appear in that part of the country for some time.

While the regiment was engaged in these services, the Irish army was defeated at Aghrim, and the city of Limerick was besieged by King William's forces. The surrender of this fortress, completed the deliverance of Ireland from the power of King James, and terminated the war in that country.

The Thirteenth regiment was relieved from garrison duty at Cork on the 22nd of December, and embarked for England, where it arrived towards the end of that month.

At this period, the desire of conquest, with the disposition, by adding city to city and province to province, to form a vast empire, and to control the nations

1692

1692 of Europe with despotic sway, marked the policy of the French court: this rendered it necessary for the British monarch to engage in war to preserve the civil and religious liberties of Europe; and while the army of the confederate states, commanded by King William, confronted the forces of Louis XIV. in the Netherlands, the THIRTEENTH were selected to form part of an expedition against the French coast, under Lieut.-General the Duke of Leinster (afterwards Duke Schomberg). The French fleet had been defeated a short time previously off La Hogue, and Louis XIV. had anticipated a descent, and had assembled so many forces on the coast, that the Duke of Leinster did not venture to land his troops. After menacing the coast of France at several points, the fleet sailed to Ostend, where the regiment landed on the 22nd of August. The THIRTEENTH and a number of other corps advanced a few stages up the country, when the French withdrew from Furnes and Dixmude, and the English took possession of, and fortified these towns.

When the army went into winter quarters, the THIRTEENTH were ordered to return to England, and they were employed on home service during the remainder of the war,

1693 After the loss of the battle of Landen, in July, 1693, by the confederate army under King William, the THIRTEENTH regiment sent a draft of one hundred and fifty men to Flanders, to replace the losses of the regiments which had suffered most on that occasion.

1695 In the early part of 1695, an accusation was preferred against Colonel Ferdinando Hastings, of charging the soldiers too high a price for certain articles which he, as Colonel, was in the habit of providing for them; an investigation afterwards took place, he was proved

REGIMENT OF LIGHT INFANTRY.   13

guilty of extortion, and deprived of his commission on 1695
the 4th of March. On the 13th of March, King William
conferred the colonelcy of the regiment on the Lieut.-
Colonel, SIR JOHN JACOB, Baronet, who had served in
it several years, and distinguished himself in Scotland
and Ireland.

In 1697 the war was terminated by the treaty of 1697
Ryswick, and King William saw his efforts to arrest the
progress of French conquests attended with complete
success. The regiment was placed upon a peace establishment in 1698; the army was further reduced in 1698
1699, and the THIRTEENTH proceeded to Ireland to 1699
replace one of the corps ordered to be disbanded in
that country.

When a powerful monarch adopts measures of un- 1700
principled aggression, and pursues schemes of aggrandizement without regard to the stipulations of treaties,
to the rights of nations, or to the privileges of individuals,
peace is not of long duration: but princes of a pacific
disposition, and people devoted to the interests of industry and commerce, are forced to assume the profession of arms, and to fight in defence of their just rights
and privileges. Such was repeatedly the case during
the reign of Louis XIV., who terminated the repose
granted to Europe by the treaty of Ryswick, by procuring the elevation of his grandson, the Duke of
Anjou, to the throne of Spain;—by taking possession
of the Spanish Netherlands,—making prisoners the
Dutch garrisons in the barrier towns, and other acts of
aggression. The interests of every state in Europe
being affected by the change in the dynasty of Spain,
the preparations for war were universal, and King
William sent thirteen British battalions to Holland, to
act as auxiliaries.

1701 The THIRTEENTH regiment was selected to proceed on foreign service : it was augmented to eight hundred and thirty officers and soldiers ; and sailing from Cork in the middle of June, 1701, arrived at Helvoetsluys, in South Holland, on the 8th of July. The British troops were afterwards sent up the Maese to Breda, and other fortified towns ; and on the 21st of September they were reviewed on Breda heath by King William III.

1702 After passing the winter in garrison in Holland, the regiment quitted its quarters on the 10th of March, 1702, and proceeded to Rosendael, where the British infantry encamped under Brigadier-General Ingoldsby, then Colonel of the 23rd Royal Welsh Fusiliers.

Colonel Sir John Jacob, Baronet, being desirous of retiring from the active duties of commanding officer of the regiment, which were performed by all colonels not having higher rank, procured permission to dispose of the coloneley of the regiment for fourteen hundred guineas, to his brother-in-law, JAMES EARL of BARRYMORE, whose appointment was dated the 15th of March, 1702, being seven days after the death of King William III., and the accession of Queen Anne.

In the middle of April, the Imperialists besieged the strong fortress of *Kayserswerth* on the Lower Rhine, and the THIRTEENTH regiment was one of the corps which traversed the country to the duchy of Cleves, and joined the covering army, under the Earl of Athlone, encamped at Cranenburg.

A French army of superior numbers proceeded, by forced marches, through the forest of Cleves and plain of Goch, to cut off the communication of the troops at Cranenburg, with Grave and *Nimeguen*. In consequence of this movement, the British and Dutch struck their tents on the evening of the 10th of June, and retreating throughout the night, arrived, about eight o'clock on 1702 the following morning, within a few miles of Nimeguen, at which time the French columns appeared on both flanks and in the rear. Some sharp skirmishing occurred: the British corps forming the rear guard behaved with great gallantry, and the army effected its retreat under the works of Nimeguen. Kayserswerth surrendered three days afterwards.

Additional forces arrived in Holland, the EARL OF MARLBOROUGH assumed the command, and the Eighth, THIRTEENTH, Seventeenth, and Eighteenth regiments, were formed in brigade under Brigadier-General Frederick Hamilton. This brigade took part in the manœuvres by which the French army was forced to withdraw from the frontiers of Holland; and when the siege of the fortress of *Venloo*—a town in the province of Limburg, situate on the east side of the Maese, with fortifications beyond the river—was undertaken, Brigadier-General Hamilton's brigade formed part of the force of thirty-two battalions of infantry and thirty-six squadrons of cavalry, detached from the main army for this enterprise, under Prince Nassau Saarbruck.

The THIRTEENTH regiment carried on its attacks against the detached fortress of *St. Michael*, on the west side of the river; and on the 18th of September, the grenadier company of the regiment was ordered to take part in storming the covered-way, which, from the extraordinary gallantry of the soldiers, ended in the capture of the fort. Between five and six o'clock in the evening the signal was given, when the grenadiers rushed forward;—the French fired a few rounds and fled;—the British leaped into the covered-way, and pursued their opponents so closely, that friends and foes entered the ravelin together. The French in the

16 THE THIRTEENTH, OR PRINCE ALBERT'S

1702 ravelin were soon sabred; those who escaped fled across a small wooden bridge, and were followed so closely that they had not time to remove the bridge, and after a sharp struggle, the English and French entered the fort together. The British got over the fausse-braye, climbed up the rampart with great difficulty,—pulled up the palisades from the parapet, ascended the rampart, and captured the fort sword in hand, making thirty officers and one hundred and seventy soldiers prisoners; the remainder of the garrison, which consisted of six hundred men, were either killed in the attack, or drowned in attempting to escape across the river, excepting twelve men, who passed the stream in small boats.

In a few days afterwards, information arrived of the capture of Landau by the Germans, when the army before Venloo assembled to fire three rounds for that event, and the batteries were ordered to fire three volleys. When the garrison and inhabitants saw the preparations in the besieging army, they imagined it was for attacking the place by storm: the magistrates begged the governor to surrender, and the town was delivered up.

After the surrender of Venloo, the THIRTEENTH regiment was engaged in the siege of *Ruremonde*, which fortress was invested towards the end of September, and surrendered on the 7th of October.

The army afterwards advanced towards *Liege;* the city was immediately delivered up, and the citadel was captured by storm on the 23rd of October: on which occasion the grenadiers of the army distinguished themselves. A detached fortress, called the Chartreuse, surrendered soon afterwards, and these conquests terminated the campaign.

REGIMENT OF LIGHT INFANTRY.   17

Quitting the valley of Liege on the 3rd of November, the regiment marched back to Holland, and was stationed in garrison at Breda during the winter. 1702

From Breda the regiment marched, in April, 1703, towards Maestricht. The French attempted to surprise the British troops in their quarters, but the gallant resistance of two regiments, at Tongres (the second, or Queen's Royals, and Elst's), gave time for the army to assemble in order of battle at Maestricht. The regiment served this campaign in brigade with the same corps as in 1702: it was employed in several movements designed to bring the enemy to a general engagement; but the French withdrew behind their fortified lines, where the DUKE OF MARLBOROUGH was desirous of attacking them, to which the Dutch generals would not consent. 1703

In August, the fortress of *Huy*, situate on the Maese above the city of Liege, was besieged, and it was captured in ten days. Another proposal to attack the French lines having been declined by the Dutch, *Limburg*, in the Spanish Netherlands, was besieged, and on the 27th of September, the garrison surrendered, which completed the deliverance of Spanish Guelderland from the power of France.

After taking part in these captures, the regiment was selected to transfer its services from the Netherlands to Portugal, to take part in the attempt to place Archduke Charles of Austria on the throne of Spain by force of arms; several states of Europe having acknowledged him as king of Spain, the British, Dutch, and Portuguese had engaged to aid him in gaining possession of the throne. The regiment embarked from Holland in October, and sailed to Portsmouth; but it was detained so long by contrary winds, that it did not

c

1704 arrive at Lisbon, before March, 1704, when it landed, and marched to Abrantes; but was afterwards removed to the Alemtejo.

The British troops in Portugal were commanded by General Mainhard Duke Schomberg, and he suggested active measures; but tardiness and inability were manifested by the Portuguese authorities, to so great an extent, that the Duke of Berwick invaded Portugal with a French and Spanish army, before the allies were prepared to take the field. The court of Lisbon was alarmed; Duke Schomberg solicited to be recalled; and the Earl of Galway was sent with reinforcements to Portugal.

In the early part of the campaign, the THIRTEENTH foot were employed in the Alemtejo: they were reviewed at the camp at Estremos on the 21st of July, and were afterwards removed to Vimiera.

After the summer heat had abated, the regiment joined the army, and penetrated into Spain as far as the bank of the Agueda, near Ciudad Rodrigo; but the Duke of Berwick had made so skilful a disposition of the French and Spanish forces under his orders, on the opposite side of the river, that the allies were prevented passing the stream, and the British troops returned to Portugal for winter quarters.

In the meantime the important fortress of *Gibraltar** had been captured by the combined English and Dutch fleets, and garrisoned by a body of marines under the Prince of Hesse Darmstadt. The capture of this fortress revived the hopes and expectations of the allies,

---

* When the Moors invaded Spain, about the year 711, they took possession of this rock, as a suitable place for the reception of supplies from the opposite coast, and they called it, in honour of a leader named TARIF, *Gib-el-tarif*, or Tarif's Mountain; hence the name of *Gibraltar* is derived

and disconcerted the measures of King Philip, of 1704 Spain, and his grandfather Louis XIV.; a combined French and Spanish army was assembled to retake Gibraltar, and the French monarch, who possessed, at that period, a naval force of great magnitude, directed his fleet to co-operate in this service. The troops under the Prince of Hesse Darmstadt defended the fortress with great gallantry, and eventually applied to the commander of the forces in Portugal for aid, when a battalion of the first and second foot guards, the THIRTEENTH and thirty-fifth regiments, the Dutch regiment of Waes, and the Portuguese regiment of Algarve, were selected to reinforce the garrison.

The THIRTEENTH regiment, mustering thirty-nine serjeants, thirty-nine corporals, twenty-six drummers, and six hundred and fifty private soldiers, marched from the frontiers of Portugal to Lisbon, and embarked on board of transports on the 8th of December: two days afterwards the fleet sailed under the convoy of four frigates, and on the 17th it was becalmed, when the boats were hoisted out, and attempts made to gain some progress by the use of oars. A fleet of men of war appeared in sight, under English and Dutch colours, and it was supposed to be the squadron under Vice-Admiral Leake and Rear-Admiral Vander-Dussen; but observing the men-of-war forming a half-moon to surround the transports, a private signal was made, and the men-of-war being unable to answer it, instantly hoisted French colours. The danger was great, with a hostile fleet so near, but the transports put out every boat, and made some way by towing: the enemy was becalmed, and in the evening a breeze sprung up, which enabled the British vessels to escape, excepting one ship, which was captured. On the fol-

1704 lowing day, the THIRTEENTH regiment landed at Gibraltar, at the moment when the garrison was beginning to despair of assistance.

The regiment was not long at Gibraltar before it had opportunities of distinguishing itself, and a detachment formed part of the body of troops which issued from the fortress during the night of the 22nd of December, forced the Spanish posts, routed a body of cavalry, levelled part of the works, burnt many fascines and gabions, and retired with little loss.

1705 Still anticipating success, the French and Spaniards prosecuted the siege; and, in the beginning of February, 1705, a chosen band of French grenadiers attacked the round tower: they climbed the rock by the aid of hooks, but were repulsed with loss.

About four days afterwards, six hundred select French and Walloon grenadiers, supported by a large body of Spaniards, ascended the hill with great silence in the night, and concealed themselves until daybreak on the morning of the 7th of February; and when the night-guard had been withdrawn from the breach near the round tower, they made a sudden rush, and drove the ordinary guard from its post with a shower of hand-grenades: at the same time, two hundred grenadiers attacked the round tower. The troops in garrison were soon alarmed, and Captain Fisher, of the Queen's marines (now fourth foot), charged the enemy at the head of seventeen men; but his party was soon overpowered and himself taken prisoner. Major MONCALL of the THIRTEENTH foot, a most gallant officer, collected between four and five hundred men, principally of his own regiment, and charged the enemy, sword in hand, so vigorously, that he soon drove them back, recaptured the round tower, after it had been in the possession of

the enemy about an hour, and liberated Captain Fisher 1705
and several other prisoners. The soldiers of the
THIRTEENTH regiment were aided, in this gallant effort,
by Colonel Rivett of the foot guards, who climbed the
rock on the right of the covered way with twenty
grenadiers, and favoured Major Moncall's success.
Additional men were brought forward, and the French
and Walloon grenadiers were driven from the works
with severe loss. On the following day, the brave
Major Moncall of the THIRTEENTH lost his leg by a
cannon-shot.

The French and Spaniards continued their unavailing
attempts on Gibraltar, and the siege became a subject
of great interest throughout Europe; but towards the
end of March, they withdrew the shattered remains of
their formidable army from before the place, and left
the English in quiet possession of the fortress they had
so gallantly defended, and which they have preserved
to the present period.

In a few weeks after the siege of Gibraltar was raised,
an expedition sailed from England, under Charles Earl
of Peterborough, either to aid the Duke of Savoy in
driving the French out of Italy, to make an attempt
on Sicily and Naples, or to further the progress of
Archduke Charles in Spain, as should appear most
advantageous for Her Majesty's service; and the latter
course was adopted. The expedition arrived at Gibraltar in the beginning of August; and the THIRTEENTH
foot were relieved from duty in that garrison by a
newly-raised regiment from England, and embarked on
board the fleet, which put to sea in a few days afterwards.

The expedition appeared off the coast of Valencia:
a thousand Catalonians and Valencians threw off their

1705 allegiance to King Philip, acknowledged Archduke Charles as sovereign of Spain, and seized on Denia, while others made demonstrations of giving effectual aid to the expedition. Thus encouraged, the Earl of Peterborough undertook the daring enterprise of besieging *Barcelona*, the capital of Catalonia, which assumed a romantic character, in consequence of his being unable to bring more than seven thousand men into the lines, the garrison consisting of nearly six thousand men, and of this fortress having resisted a French army of thirty thousand men, eight weeks, in 1697, and cost the French monarch twelve thousand men to take it. The troops landed on the 23rd and 24th of August, and the THIRTEENTH regiment took part in the siege. On the 13th of September, the grenadier company of the regiment left the camp, and after a night march among the mountains, appeared before the detached fortress of *Montjuich*, at daylight on the following morning, and took part in storming the outworks of that place, in which it had several men killed and wounded. Three days afterwards, the strong castle and citadel of Montjuich surrendered, which greatly facilitated the progress of the siege of Barcelona.

The besieging army was so very weak in numbers that extraordinary efforts were necessary: the soldiers and seamen were incessant in their exertions; cannon and mortars were dragged up steep precipices by men, and a practicable breach having been made, a detachment of the THIRTEENTH foot was in readiness to take part in storming the works, when the governor surrendered.

The capture of so important a fortress, by so small a body of men, produced a great sensation throughout Europe, and this splendid achievement was followed by

the submission of nearly all Catalonia, the largest and 1705
richest province of Spain.

Elated by this success, the Earl of Peterborough resolved to undertake another enterprise of a more romantic character than the former, namely the invasion of Valencia, with a body of troops not sufficiently numerous to form the advance guard of the opposing army. The THIRTEENTH regiment being conspicuous for its efficiency, and for the gallant bearing of the officers and soldiers, was selected to form part of his Lordship's force.

From Barcelona the regiment marched under the command of Lieut.-Col. EDWARD PEARCE, to Tortosa, on the river Ebro. In the meantime the Conde de las Torres having been sent by King Philip, with a numerous force, to retake the towns which had declared for Archduke Charles, he had besieged the fortress of *St. Matheo*, and the THIRTEENTH were ordered to march to the relief of this town. The troops employed in this service were very inferior in numbers to the besieging army; but by night marches among the woods and mountains, and circulating exaggerated reports of his numbers, the British general succeeded in surprising his opponents, and the Spanish commander, being deceived by spies, made a precipitate retreat.

After this service was performed, the officers and men were so exhausted by long marches, day and night over the mountains, that the regiment was ordered into quarters of refreshment at Vinaros, where it remained a short period, while the Earl of Peterborough was making preparations for the expedition to Valencia.

Early in the year 1706, Lieut.-Col. Pearce received 1706 orders to march with the THIRTEENTH regiment from Vinaros to Oropeso, where an extraordinary alteration

1706 took place in the character of the corps, which is without parallel in the history of the British army. The Earl of Peterborough was much in want of cavalry for his expedition to Valencia, and he procured, with great zeal and industry, about eight hundred Spanish horses; about two hundred of these horses were given to the Royal Dragoons, and other corps, to remount the men whose horses had died, and with the other six hundred he resolved to form a corps of cavalry. He had been much pleased with the conduct of the THIRTEENTH foot on all occasions, and he determined to constitute them a *Regiment of Dragoons.* This was, however, not communicated to the officers and soldiers until every preparation was made, and as the regiment approached Oropeso, it was met by the Earl of Peterborough, and reviewed on a small plain near the town. After the review the horses were produced, and the regiment was constituted a corps of dragoons of eight troops, of which Lieut.-Col. Edward Pearce was appointed colonel. The following account of this circumstance is copied from Dr. Freind's account of the Earl of Peterborough's campaign in Valencia:—' No surprise, I believe, was
' equal to that of the officers and soldiers of Colonel
' Pearce's regiment, who had orders to march from
' Vinaros, to a place called Oropeso, four leagues from
' Castillon de la Plana: at this place, by ten in the
' morning, they were met by the Earl of Peterborough,
' on a plain just bordering on the town. His Lordship
' having made a review, was complimenting the regi-
' ment, and wishing he had horses and accoutrements,
' to try whether a corps of so good a character would
' maintain the like reputation upon such a change.
' They, no doubt, concurred very heartily with his
' Lordship in his wishes, little expecting the execution

'of them in a moment: but his Lordship having 1706
' ordered his secretary to give the commissions already
' prepared, the officers at last believed the general in
' earnest; when, turning to the edge of a hill, they
' saw eight bodies of horses, drawn up separately, and
' found them all ready accoutred. Among these there
' were three good horses for each captain, two for each
' lieutenant, and one for each cornet. My Lord left to
' the field officers the choice of their troops; the other
' captains drew lots : and immediately they all mounted
' and marched to the quarters appointed for them.'

In the 'Annals of Queen Anne,' it is stated:—' He
' (the Earl of Peterborough) collected above six
' hundred horses, with which he recruited his horse, and
' formed a regiment of dragoons of the LORD BARRY-
' MORE's regiment of foot, the command of which new
regiment he gave to Lieut.-Col. Pearce, ordering the
' remaining officers of the old corps to return to England
' to recruit the same.'

Similar statements to the above are contained in Carleton's Memoirs, Tindal's History of England, and other historical works. In the official records, it is stated, that twenty-seven officers and six hundred and sixty non-commissioned officers and soldiers of the THIRTEENTH foot, then called the Earl of Barrymore's regiment, were formed into a corps of dragoons in Spain; that Lieut.-Col. Pearce of the THIRTEENTH was appointed colonel of the new regiment of dragoons, which obtained rank in the army from the 25th of February, 1706; and that 900*l.* levy money was paid for recruiting the THIRTEENTH to its establishment in England.

The regiment of dragoons thus formed proved a valuable corps, and distinguished itself on several occasions. It formed part of the force engaged in the

1706 Earl of Peterborough's splendid campaign in Valencia, and evinced great gallantry in the capturing of the Spanish battering train near the city of Valencia. After the siege of Barcelona was raised, this regiment advanced upon Madrid, and joined the army of Portugal, under the Earl of Galway, at Guadalaxara, on the 8th of August, 1706. It subsequently took part in covering the march of the army to Valencia, and was so reduced in numbers by continual service, and the losses it sustained in numerous skirmishes, that in the spring of 1707, it only mustered two hundred and seventy-three men. It was one of the corps which displayed great intrepidity and bravery at the battle of Almanza, on the 25th of April, 1707, when it had Lieut.-Col. Deloches, Cornets Cundy and Holmes, and Quarter-Master Sturges killed; Lieut. Fitzgerald and Cornet Barry wounded and taken prisoners: it also sustained a severe loss in killed and wounded. It was disbanded after the treaty of Utrecht in 1713.

The remaining officers and soldiers of the THIRTEENTH, who were not constituted dragoons, returned to England in 1706, and had so great success in recruiting the regiment, that in less than two years it was fit for service.

1707 While the regiment was recruiting in England, the allied army was defeated at Almanza, and a French and Spanish force invaded Portuguese Estremadura and the Alemtejo, when four regiments (the fifth, twentieth, thirty-ninth, and Stanwix's, afterwards disbanded) embarked from Ireland for Portugal; and during the winter the THIRTEENTH regiment, being again fit for duty, proceeded to the same destination: it was placed on the strength of the army in Portugal on the 24th of December, 1707.

1708 After landing at Lisbon, the regiment marched under

REGIMENT OF LIGHT INFANTRY. 27

the orders of its colonel, the Earl of Barrymore, to the 1708
Alemtejo; in the spring of 1708 it was encamped at
Fuentes de Sapatores, between Elvas and Campo Mayor,
with the army commanded by the Marquis de Fronteira,
and was formed in brigade with the regiments of
Stanwix and Galway (newly-raised corps, afterwards
disbanded) under Brigadier-General Thomas Pearce
(of the fifth foot); but the services of the THIRTEENTH
were limited to operations of a defensive character.

In April, 1709, the regiment was encamped near 1709
Estremos, from whence it was removed to Elvas, and
subsequently to the banks of the Caya. On the 7th
of May, the French and Spaniards under the Marquis
de Bay marched in the direction of Campo Mayor,
when the Portuguese generals resolved to pass the *Caya*
and attack the enemy, contrary to the advice of
the Earl of Galway. The Portuguese cavalry of the
right wing crossed the river, and opened a sharp
cannonade; but when the opposing horsemen advanced
to charge, the Portuguese squadron galloped out of the
field, leaving their cannon behind. The infantry of
the allied army stood its ground, repulsed the charges
of the Spanish cavalry three times, and afterwards commenced its retreat, when the Earl of Galway led forward
the THIRTEENTH, Stanwix's, and his own regiment, to
favour the retrograde movement. The THIRTEENTH
were in front, and charged the Spaniards with distin-
tinguished gallantry; the other two regiments of the
brigade also evinced great bravery, and the three corps
overthrew the leading columns of the opposing army,
and recaptured the Portuguese guns. Animated and
encouraged by this success, the three regiments pressed
forward until they became exposed to the attack of
superior numbers, when the Portuguese cavalry of the

1709 left wing were ordered to support them, but instead of obeying these orders, the Portuguese squadrons galloped to the rear. Thus forsaken, the three regiments were cut off from the allied army, surrounded by opponents, and only a few officers and men were able to cut their passage through the host of adversaries which environed them; the remainder were forced to surrender prisoners of war. Among the prisoners were Major-General Sankey and Brigadier-General Thomas Pearce.

The THIRTEENTH foot sustained a severe loss on this occasion; besides the killed and wounded, it had Colonel the Earl of Barrymore, four aptains, eight lieutenants, eight ensigns, three volunteers, and between two and three hundred non-commissioned officers and soldiers taken prisoners.

1710 The captured officers and soldiers were exchanged; and the regiment served the campaign of 1710 on the frontiers of Portugal, but had no opportunity of distinguishing itself.

1711 In 1711 the THIRTEENTH foot were withdrawn from Portugal, and proceeded to Gibraltar, where they
1713 were stationed until the peace of Utrecht, 1713, when that fortress was ceded to Great Britain.

At the conclusion of the peace, 1713, the regiment received drafts of non-commissioned officers and soldiers from several corps which were ordered to be disbanded, and the protection of the important fortress of Gibraltar was confided to the fifth, THIRTEENTH, and twentieth regiments.

1715 On the 8th July, 1715, the Earl of Barrymore was succeeded in the command of the regiment by Colonel Stanhope Cotton, who had served in Brigadier-General Bowles's regiment, which was disbanded in 1713.

REGIMENT OF LIGHT INFANTRY.   29

Colonel Cotton was honoured with the appointment 1715 of Lieut.-Governor of Gibraltar, and the THIRTEENTH regiment, under his command, was as much distinguished for its excellent conduct in garrison in time of peace, as it had been for its gallantry in action during the war.

After commanding the regiment upwards of twelve 1725 years, Colonel Cotton died on the 7th of December, 1725, when King George I. conferred the colonelcy of the THIRTEENTH foot on Brigadier-General Lord Mark Kerr, from the twenty-ninth regiment.

The importance of *Gibraltar* had rendered the 1726 loss of that fortress a subject of deep regret to the crown of Spain, and on the prospect of England being involved in a continental war, in 1726, the Spanish monarch resolved to commence hostilities with Great Britain, by a determined effort to recover possession of this desirable entrepôt to the Mediterranean, which gave the THIRTEENTH regiment another opportunity of adding to its honours, that of a second successful defence of Gibraltar.

The Spaniards made preparations for the siege upon 1727 an extensive scale : their troops encamped before the fortress in January, 1727, under General Count de las Torres, and the bringing up of cannon and mortars occupied several weeks. In February they commenced constructing batteries, before any declaration of war had been made, and persisted in the work, notwithstanding the remonstrances of the Lieut.-Governor, Colonel Jasper Clayton.

On the 21st of February, the garrison opened its fire upon the besiegers, and from that day the thunder of cannon and mortars reverberated among the mountains of Andalusia, proclaiming the strenuous efforts of the besieging army, and the gallant defence made by the

1727 garrison, which was encouraged by the arrival of additional corps from England. The siege was continued until thousands of Spaniards had perished in the attempt; but very little loss had been sustained by the garrison. In the early part of June the fire slackened, and on the 18th of that month hostilities ceased, in consequence of preliminary articles for a treaty of peace having been agreed upon.

1728 The regiment was relieved from duty at Gibraltar in the spring of 1728, and returning to England, after an absence of upwards of twenty years, landed at Portsmouth on the 1st of May.

1730 On the 18th of July, 1730, King George II. reviewed the regiment, in brigade with the twelfth foot, on Winkfield plain. His Majesty was accompanied by the Queen, and a number of distinguished persons, and the appearance and movements of the two regiments excited great admiration.

1732 In May, 1732, Lord Mark Kerr was removed to the eleventh dragoons, and was succeeded in the colonelcy of the THIRTEENTH foot, by Colonel John Middleton, from the twenty-fifth regiment. This officer commanded the regiment seven years, and died on the 4th

1739 of May, 1739: the colonelcy remained vacant two months, and was conferred, on the 5th of July, on Colonel Henry Pulteney from major of the second foot guards.

On the 23rd of October of this year war was proclaimed against Spain, and the establishment of the regiment was augmented to eight hundred and fifteen officers and soldiers.

1740 In the summer of 1740 the THIRTEENTH foot pitched their tents in Windsor forest, where an encampment of two regiments of horse, three of dragoons, and three of foot, was formed, under Lieut.-General Honeywood. In the autumn of this year, Charles VI. Emperor of

Germany died, when the succession of the Archduchess 1740
Maria Theresa, as Queen of Hungary and Bohemia,
was disputed by the Elector of Bavaria, who was supported by the arms of France.

On the prospect of Great Britain being involved in 1741
the war on the Continent, the regiment was held in
readiness to embark for foreign service, and in July,
1741, it pitched its tents on Lexden-heath, in the county
of Essex, where three regiments of horse, four of dragoons, and seven of foot, were encamped, and held in
readiness to proceed abroad.

In the summer of 1742, sixteen thousand men pro- 1742
ceeded to Flanders, under the Earl of Stair, to support the house of Austria: the THIRTEENTH regiment
was one of the corps which proceeded to Flanders,
where it remained in quarters until the early part of
the following year. On the 31st March, 1743, war was 1743
declared against France, and the troops which the King
of Great Britain had assembled in the Netherlands
began their march for Germany. The THIRTEENTH
was engaged in operations in the territory bordering
on the Rhine, and after several movements it was encamped at Aschaffenburg, where King George II. and
His Royal Highness the Duke of Cumberland joined
the army.

On the 27th of June, the troops commenced their
march for Hanau, when a body of French crossed the
river Maine, and formed for battle in a strong position
near the village of *Dettingen*. The allied army formed
for action under a heavy cannonade, and about midday the contest commenced. The THIRTEENTH were
sharply engaged, and had the honour to signalize
themselves under the eye of their sovereign, who
evinced great personal bravery, and stimulated the
soldiers to deeds of heroism by his presence and ani-

1743 mating language. The French army was defeated and driven across the river Maine with severe loss, and the allied army stood triumphant on the field of battle, having in its possession many colours, standards, prisoners, and other trophies indicating a complete victory.

Twenty-one rank and file of the THIRTEENTH foot were killed on this occasion; and Ensigns Ogilbie and Gray, one drummer, and twenty-nine rank and file, wounded.

From the field of battle, the army continued its march, on the following day, to Hanau, where the regiment was encamped several weeks: it afterwards crossed the Rhine, and was engaged in operations in West Germany; but repassed the Rhine in October, and returned to Flanders for winter-quarters.

1744 In May, 1744, the regiment again took the field, and served the campaign of that year under Field-Marshal Wade: it was encamped between Asche and Alost, and afterwards on the banks of the Scheldt. Towards the end of the campaign it penetrated the territory subject to France as far as Lisle, but returned to Ghent for winter quarters.

1745 In April, 1745, the regiment pitched its tents near Brussels, and in the beginning of May marched to the village of Soignies, from whence it advanced, with the army commanded by His Royal Highness the Duke of Cumberland, to the relief of *Tournay*, which fortress was besieged by a numerous French force. This movement brought on a general engagement, near the village of *Fontenoy*, on the 11th of May, when the regiment had another opportunity of distinguishing itself in conflict with the enemy.

On this occasion the regiment entered the plain in front of the French position, formed line under a heavy fire of artillery from the enemy's batteries, and advanced to attack the formidable array of infantry and artillery posted on the right of the village of Fontenoy. The British infantry, advancing to the attack, exhibited a splendid spectacle of war, and the heroic resolution with which they precipitated themselves, with the bayonet, upon the opposing ranks, proved the innate bravery of the men; but owing to the failure of the Dutch in their attack on the village, the British were forced to retire. The attack was repeated, British prowess was again triumphant, and the French lines were forced; but the Dutch failed a second time, and the British were compelled to withdraw: the army retreated from the field of battle to Aeth.

1745

Captain Queenchant, two serjeants, and thirty-five private soldiers of the THIRTEENTH foot, were killed; Captain-Lieutenant Daniel Nicholas, Lieutenants William Jones and Samuel Edhouse, two serjeants, and thirty-nine private men were wounded.

Leaving Aeth on the 16th of May, the regiment encamped on the plains of Lessines, and was afterwards employed in defensive operations; but the allied army was not sufficiently numerous to prevent the enemy obtaining possession of several fortified towns.

While the army was in Flanders, Charles Edward, eldest son of the Pretender, arrived in Scotland, and being joined by several clans, he asserted his father's pretensions to the throne. Unaccustomed to hear the sound of war at their own gates, the British people were at first alarmed, but soon recovering, they evinced loyalty and union in sustaining the fixed rights of their sovereign and in defending their own liberties. The volunteer associations were not, however, ready to take the field for some time, and several corps were ordered

1745 to return from Flanders. The THIRTEENTH regiment was one of the corps ordered home on this occasion, and it landed at Blackwall on the 23rd of September. It was immediately ordered to the north; and, joining the troops assembled by Field-Marshal Wade at Doncaster, marched from thence to Newcastle-on-Tyne. When the clans penetrated into England, the regiment was employed in covering Yorkshire, and when they made their precipitate retreat to Scotland, it returned to Newcastle, where it arrived on the 26th of December.

1746 From Newcastle the regiment marched to Edinburgh, and joined the forces assembled at that place, under Lieut.-General Hawley, for the relief of Stirling Castle, which was besieged by the young Pretender. This force advanced to *Falkirk*, where it arrived on the 16th of January, 1746, and encamped. On the following day the outposts gave information of the approach of the rebel army, and the King's troops left their camp-ground and formed for battle on Falkirk moor. At the moment when the battle commenced, a heavy storm of wind and rain beat violently in the faces of the King's troops; the soldiers could scarcely see their opponents, their muskets would not give fire, confusion ensued, and a great portion of the army retired from the field of battle: a few regiments, however, remained firm, and repulsed the left wing of the rebel army.

After retiring from Falkirk moor, the THIRTEENTH regiment marched back to Edinburgh, where additional forces arrived, and His Royal Highness the Duke of Cumberland took the command of the troops in Scotland.

On the 31st of January, the army again advanced, when the young Pretender raised the siege of Stirling

Castle, and made a precipitate retreat towards In- 1746
verness. The THIRTEENTH were engaged in the pursuit of the rebel clans; but the army was forced to halt at Perth, in consequence of the severity of the weather, until the 20th of February, when the march was resumed; and in the beginning of March, the army arrived at Aberdeen, where it was detained by heavy rain and snow storms.

In the early part of April, the King's troops were again in motion, and on the 14th of that month they arrived at Nairn. The rebels made a sudden advance from Inverness, with the view of surprising the royal forces in the night, but finding the outposts alert, they retreated.

Early on the morning of the 16th of April, the army advanced in three columns towards Inverness, and about eleven o'clock the rebel forces were discovered on *Culloden* moor, when the royal army formed for battle; the THIRTEENTH regiment having its post in Brigadier-General Mordaunt's division, and bringing into the field twenty-two officers, twenty-three serjeants, nineteen drummers, and three hundred and ten rank and file. In the first instance, the regiment formed part of the reserve, but as the army advanced, a change in the character of the ground occasioned the THIRTEENTH foot to be ordered forward to take post on the right of the royals. The fire of cannon was succeeded by several charges, in which the King's troops were victorious. A body of Highlanders, with broad swords and targets, advanced towards the THIRTEENTH foot, but they were intimidated by the gallant bearing of the regiment, and fled from the field before the soldiers could close upon them with bayonets. The rebel army was routed at every part of the field, and pursued for several miles with great

1746 slaughter, and the loss of all its artillery. Thus the events of one day transformed the young Pretender from an imaginary monarch to a destitute fugitive, and after enduring great hardship and suffering he escaped to France.

After the victory at Culloden, the regiment was encamped a short period at Inverness, and it was subsequently employed in escorting the prisoners taken on that occasion.

The rebellion in Scotland having been suppressed, the THIRTEENTH regiment was ordered to return to the Netherlands. It landed in Holland in the autumn and advanced up the country to Maestricht, where it arrived on the 9th of October. At this period, the French army under Marshal Saxe, and the allied army under Prince Charles of Lorraine, were manœuvring in the vicinity of the city of Liege, and an engagement being expected, the regiment received orders to advance with all possible expedition, and join the army. In obedience to these orders, the regiment quitted Maestricht, and, by a forced march, arrived in the vicinity of Liege on the morning of the 11th of October, at the moment when the French army was developing its attack on three villages, which were occupied by eight battalions of English, Dutch, and Hessians. The regiment was instantly ordered to take post near the village of *Roucoux*, under the command of Brigadier-General Houghton. The leading brigades of the enemy were repulsed, and a second line of combatants was defeated; but the enemy brought forward so many fresh troops, that the eight battalions were driven from the villages by superior numbers. A retreat was ordered, which was executed with great regularity, and the army marched to the vicinity of Maestricht.

The regiment was subsequently employed in the province of Limburg, and passed the winter in quarters near the Dutch frontiers.

In the spring of 1747, the regiment took the field, and formed part of the army under the command of His Royal Highness the Duke of Cumberland. After encamping for a short period near the banks of the Scheldt, it was employed in operations on the Great Nethe and on the Demer. On the 1st of July, the opposing armies confronted each other between Tongres and Maestricht, and the THIRTEENTH, twenty-fifth, and thirty-seventh regiments, with Freudeman's Hanoverians, and a portion of artillery, took possession of the village of *Val*, situate about a league from Maestricht, and on the south of the road from that place to Tongres. The day was passed in cannonading and skirmishing, and the troops lay all the night on their arms.

Early on the morning of the 2nd of July, the French infantry descended the hills, and advanced in a grand column of upwards of sixty battalions against the village of Val, where the THIRTEENTH and three other regiments were formed to resist this immense array of French power, and the Duke of Cumberland galloped to that part of the field to encourage the soldiers to a determined resistance, and to be ready to support them as circumstances might require. About ten o'clock, the French artillery opened a heavy fire, and the second shot killed the Duke of Cumberland's German aide-de-camp, Baron Ziggesaer: under the cover of this cannonade, the leading brigade of the French column attacked the village, and the British battalions withstood the tempest of war with astonishing firmness, repulsing the French regiments, and driving

1747

1747 them back with severe loss. As the discomfited regiments retired, a second line of combatants advanced to storm the village, but they were met, overthrown, and driven back in disorder, and the THIRTEENTH and other regiments at that point remained triumphant at their post. Few moments elapsed before a fresh body of assailants came rushing forward, but the British battalions were again victorious; and a fourth attack on the village was also repulsed. The French commander appeared determined to carry this point, and his superior numbers enabling him to continue to send forward fresh troops, he eventually gained possession of the village; but the THIRTEENTH, and other corps which had occupied that post, were reinforced by four additional battalions, and they returned to the charge, and recovered the village in gallant style. The vicinity of *Val* was covered with killed and wounded men, and several French brigades had been nearly destroyed, yet the French commander continued to order forward fresh troops: the soldiers on both sides fought with great resolution, and the village was lost and won several times.

The superior numbers of his army gave Marshal Saxe a decided advantage, and after the display of British valour, which reflected great honor on the corps engaged, the army was ordered to retreat towards Maestricht.

In the narratives of this battle published at the time, the heroic conduct of the corps engaged is highly commended. The THIRTEENTH foot had Lieutenant Haddock and forty rank and file killed; Captain Stafford, Lieutenant Naylor, Ensign Holyday, five serjeants, two drummers, and seventy rank and file wounded; fifty-one non-commissioned officers and soldiers prisoners of war and missing.

The regiment was employed near the frontiers of the 1747
United Provinces during the remainder of the campaign,
but it was not again engaged in combat with the enemy.

A fine body of recruits from England replaced the
losses of the preceding year, and in the spring of 1748, 1748
the regiment again took the field, and was employed in
several services in the province of Limburg and in North
Brabant. Preliminary articles for a treaty of peace
were afterwards agreed upon, a suspension of hostilities
took place, and the regiment went into quarters in
Holland.

A treaty of peace, concluded at Aix-la-Chapelle,
terminated the contest, and during the winter the regiment returned to England.

In 1749 a reduction was made in the strength of the 1749
army, and the THIRTEENTH regiment was placed on a
peace establishment.

On the 1st of July, 1751, King George II. issued 1751
a regulation relative to the clothing, standards, and
colours of the several regiments. According to this
regulation, the uniform of the THIRTEENTH regiment
was scarlet, faced and lined with *philemot yellow*. The
first, or King's, colour was the great union; the second
colour was of philemot yellow silk, with the union in
the upper canton, and in the centre of the colour, XIII.
in gold Roman characters, within a wreath of roses and
thistles on the same stalk.

The regiment remained in Great Britain until the 1754
year 1754, when it embarked for Gibraltar; and was
stationed at that fortress during the whole of the seven
years' war; at the termination of hostilities in 1762, 1762
it returned to England.

King George III. paid great attention to everything 1766
connected with the army, and the THIRTEENTH foot

40 THE THIRTEENTH, OR PRINCE ALBERT'S

1766 obtained His Majesty's special approbation of their conduct on all occasions. In June, 1766, His Royal Highness William, DUKE OF GLOUCESTER, was appointed colonel of the regiment, in succession to General the Honorable Henry Pulteney, who resigned.

1767 His Majesty reviewed the regiment in Hyde Park, in brigade with the twelfth foot, on the 5th of June, 1767: the Queen, and a numerous assemblage of distinguished persons, were present on this occasion; and the King was pleased to express his high approbation of the appearance and discipline of the two corps.

In December the Duke of Gloucester was promoted to the rank of major-general, and appointed colonel of the third foot guards; at the same time the colonelcy of the THIRTEENTH foot was conferred on Major-General the Honorable James Murray, from colonel-commandant in the sixtieth regiment.

1768 After remaining in England upwards of five years, the THIRTEENTH were ordered to transfer their services to Ireland, where they arrived in August, 1768, and were stationed in that part of the United Kingdom seven months.

1769 In March, 1769, the regiment embarked for the island of Minorca.

1775 When the American war commenced, in 1775, the regiment was performing garrison duty at Port Mahon; it was relieved, soon afterwards by a battalion of Hanoverians, which had been taken into British pay, and re-
1776 turned to England, where it arrived in February, 1776.

1778 In the summer of 1778, the regiment was encamped near Plymouth, with four battalions of militia, under Lieut.-General Parker.

1779 The regiment was encamped, in 1779, at Rye; and,
1780 in 1780, pitched its tents at Dorking.

REGIMENT OF LIGHT INFANTRY. 41

Meanwhile the American war had been continued; 178
France and Spain had taken part in the contest, in
favour of the colonists; and an English armament
had captured several French islands in the West
Indies. The enemy sent a powerful force to recap-
ture the lost possessions; and, in 1781, the THIR-
TEENTH received orders to proceed to the Leeward
Islands, to augment the British force in that part of
His Majesty's dominions.

Soon after the regiment arrived in the West Indies, 1782
hostilities were terminated; the British Monarch
acceded to the independence of the United States, and a
treaty of peace was concluded. This change occasioned
the regiment to return to England in 1782.

In this year, the THIRTEENTH foot received directions
to assume the title of the FIRST SOMERSETSHIRE REGI-
MENT, and, in order to facilitate the procuring of recruits,
to cultivate a connection between that county and the
regiment.

The army was reduced in 1783, when the regiment 1783
was placed upon a peace establishment.

In the spring of 1784, the regiment embarked for 1784
Ireland, where it was quartered during the succeeding
six years.

On the 5th of June, 1789, General the Honorable 1789
James Murray was removed to the twenty-first foot,
or Royal North British Fusiliers, and His Majesty conferred the colonelcy of the THIRTEENTH regiment on
Major-General George Ainslie, from the lieut.-colon-
elcy of the fifteenth light dragoons.

In the following year, the regiment received orders 1790
to hold itself in readiness for foreign service. A revolution had taken place in France; the French monarch
was divested of regal power; the doctrines of liberty

1790 and equality were disseminated, and Great Britain was on the eve of being engaged in a contest to arrest the destructive operation of the principles of democracy.

The doctrines of equality were taught in the French West India Islands; their mischievous tendency was soon experienced among the black population, and the British Government deeming it necessary to augment its military power in that part of the world, the THIRTEENTH regiment was sent as a reinforcement to the island of Jamaica.

1791 In 1791, the negroes of the French settlements in *St. Domingo*, (now the black republic of Hayti) one of the largest and most fertile of the West India Islands, revolted; the island became a scene of massacre and devastation, and the French planters solicited the aid of the British, in 1793; when troops were sent to enable them to recover their estates from their former slaves. The revolted blacks and mulattoes took possession of part of the island, and declared themselves a free and independent people: the British gained several important posts; many of the planters transferred their allegiance to the British crown, and strenuous efforts were made to deliver the island from the domination
1793 of the slaves. Towards the end of 1793, the THIRTEENTH regiment embarked from Jamaica, and proceeded to the island of St. Domingo, where it was engaged in many difficult and arduous services, in which the officers and soldiers evinced valour, constancy, and patient endurance of the most distressing sufferings, in a manner which reflected great credit on the corps.

1794 In January, 1794, the regiment was stationed at Jeremie, of which town its commanding officer, Lieut.- Colonel John Whitelocke, was commandant. On the 31st of January, the regiment embarked, with the expedition commanded by Lieut.-Colonel Whitelocke, 1794 for the attack of the important post of Cape *Tiburon*, which commanded Cape Nichola mole, and an extensive bay. On the evening of the 2nd of February, the squadron approached the shore, where about six hundred and fifty blacks, and two hundred mulattoes and whites were formed to oppose the landing. A few broadsides from the frigates soon cleared the beach, and as the sun was declining beneath the horizon, Major Brent Spencer, of the THIRTEENTH, quitted the ships with the flank companies of the expedition. As the boats approached the shore, a line of opponents commenced a sharp fire of musketry; but the soldiers leaped upon the beach, charged with bayonets, routed their opponents in an instant, killed and wounded a number of blacks and mulattoes, and took possession of a house which was well situated for protecting the landing of the whole of the detachment. At daylight on the following morning, the THIRTEENTH and twentieth regiments landed, with a party of marines and of the British Legion; and as the troops prepared to attack the post, the enemy fled, leaving twenty-two pieces of heavy ordnance, three field-pieces, and a magazine full of every description of ammunition, behind them : about fifty of the enemy were killed and wounded, and a hundred and fifty taken prisoners.

The loss of the regiment, on this occasion, was limited to two private soldiers killed; Captain the Honorable Charles Colville, Lieutenant George Kinnaird Dana, Volunteer Dolphina, and two private soldiers, wounded. The conduct of Major Spencer of the THIRTEENTH, and of the officers and soldiers of the flank companies, was commended in Lieut.-Colonel Whitelocke's despatch.

1794 This important post was placed under the charge of Lieutenant Robert Baskerville, of the THIRTEENTH, who had fifty men of his own regiment, the colonial corps, and Jean Kino's corps from Irois, under his orders for the defence of the post.

On the 20th of February, the flank companies of the THIRTEENTH were engaged in the storming of the post of *L'Acal*, situate six miles from Leogane. Part of the force designed for this service proceeded by water, and the remainder by land : the whole under Lieut.-Colonel Whitelocke. Contrary winds prevented the troops in transports taking part in the attack, but the other division captured the fort in gallant style ; the soldiers climbing the hill, exposed to a heavy fire of grape and musketry, and their progress impeded by felled trees placed in all directions, and capturing the works with fixed bayonets. After obtaining possession of the fort, two officers and thirteen soldiers were killed by the explosion of a magazine. The only loss sustained by the THIRTEENTH foot was one private soldier killed; one serjeant, and one private soldier wounded. Major Spencer again distinguished himself.

The flank companies of the regiment were employed, under Brigadier-General Whyte, in the expedition against *Port-au-Prince*, the capital of the island : the troops employed in this service arrived in the bay on the 31st of May, and the capture of this place was accomplished in four days, with little loss. A malignant fever broke out in the town soon afterwards, and the British lost forty officers and six hundred soldiers by disease, within two months after the surrender of the place. Lieut.-Colonel Whitelocke had the rank of colonel in the expedition, and Major Spencer that of lieut.-colonel ; they both distinguished themselves, and their conduct was commended in the strongest terms in Brigadier-General Whyte's despatch. {1794}

Captain James Grant, of the THIRTEENTH regiment, commanded the garrison of *Fort Bizzeton*, which consisted of one hundred and twenty men. Between four and five o'clock on the morning of the 5th of December, three columns of the enemy, amounting to about two thousand men, approached the fort with great silence, and arrived under the works before they were discovered; but the garrison was under arms; it repulsed the assailants, and drove them from before the works with great loss. Major-General Sir Adam Williamson stated in his public despatch,—' Captain ' Grant (THIRTEENTH), and his two lieutenants, Clunes ' of the Royals, and Hamilton of the twenty-second ' regiment, merit every attention that can be shown ' them. They were all three severely wounded early ' in the attack, but tied up their wounds and continued ' to defend their post. It has been a very gallant ' defence and does them great honor.'

The regiment continued actively employed in St. Domingo in the year 1795; but the climate proved particularly injurious to the health of the officers and soldiers, and its losses from disease were so severe that, in 1796, it returned to England a skeleton. {1795} {1796}

After remaining in England a few months, the regiment embarked for Ireland in 1797, and arrived in that part of the kingdom at the period when the Roman Catholics were combining against the British government, and preparing for open rebellion, in the expectation of receiving aid from France. {1797}

In May, 1798, the rebellion broke out, and the passions of the misguided peasantry having been excited {1798}

1798 into a state of fury, by all the motives which bigotry and vengeance could inspire, their conduct was marked by actions of a most atrocious and cruel character. The THIRTEENTH regiment was, however, weak in numbers, and it was not called in very active service on this occasion. The rebellion was suppressed towards the end of July; and in August, when a body of French troops arrived, they were surrounded and made prisoners.

1799 The regiment remained in Ireland recruiting its numbers during the year 1799.

1800 In the early part of 1800, the establishment was completed by volunteers from the Irish militia; and on the 3rd of March the regiment embarked for England, where it arrived, a splendid corps of disciplined men, and it was soon afterwards selected to proceed on foreign service.

The Spanish monarch had united with France, in the war against Great Britain, and an attack on the ports of Spain formed part of the plan for employing the disposable force of the country. The THIRTEENTH embarked from England on the 31st of July, and sailed, with the expedition under Lieut.-General Sir James Pulteney, to the bay of Corunna, and a landing was effected on the coast of Galicia, with the design of attacking the fortress of *Ferrol;* but after viewing the town and its defences, Sir James Pulteney resolved not to lose time in attacking this place, and the troops re-embarked and proceeded to join General Sir Ralph Abercromby, who commanded a British force in the Mediterranean. The united forces appeared before *Cadiz,* and summoned the governor to surrender; but a disease was ravaging the city at the time, and the fleet quitted the coast for fear of infection, and proceeded to Gibraltar.

At this period a veteran French army, which had 1800
been vauntingly styled the '*Army of the East*,' was
holding *Egypt* in subjection, and meditating scenes of
conquest in distant regions; and the British government resolved to employ the disposable force of the
kingdom in delivering Egypt from the French yoke.
The THIRTEENTH, commanded by Lieut.-Colonel
the Honorable Charles Colville, were selected for
this enterprise : they mustered seven hundred and
thirty-seven rank and file, fit for duty, and formed part
of the second brigade under Major-General Cradock.

After experiencing much severe weather at sea, the
fleet arrived at the island of Malta, where the troops
went on shore, and the abundance of fresh provisions
which the island afforded, with the comforts of the
beautiful city of Valetta, soon restored and reani-
mated the troops.

Leaving Malta on the 20th of December, the armament sailed to Marmorice, in Asiatic Turkey, where
the fleet anchored in a spacious bay surrounded by
mountains, while gun-boats were being procured for
the expedition, horses for the cavalry, and a plan of
co-operation arranged with the Turks.

On the 23rd of February, 1801, the fleet again put 1801
to sea, and arriving off Alexandria on the 1st of March,
bore down at sunset into the bay of *Aboukir*. On the
morning of the 8th of March, as the rays of light gilded
the horizon, one hundred and fifty boats laden with soldiers approached the shore, which was crowded with
French troops assembled to oppose the landing. The
murmuring sound of a thousand oars, urging forward
the *élite* of a brave army, whose arms glittered in the
rays of the morning sun, was soon lost in the loud
thunder of cannon, and a storm of bullets from the

1801 shore cut furrows in the surface of the water; a few boats were struck and began to sink, others stopped to save the men, and a momentary check was given; but the impulse returned with increased ardour, and pressing through the storm of grape and musketry, the rowers forced their boats to the beach. The soldiers instantly leaped on the shore, formed as they advanced, and rushing up the heights with supernatural energy, charged with bayonets, and overthrew the opposing ranks. A sharp combat ensued; the THIRTEENTH regiment landed during the action, and the French were driven from their position, with the loss of three hundred men, eight pieces of cannon, and many horses. Thus was the first step gained towards the accomplishment of this brilliant enterprise; and the landing on the shores of Egypt ranks among the splendid achievements of the British arms.

Advancing towards *Alexandria*, the troops arrived, on the 12th of March, at the vicinity of Mandora Tower, and on the succeeding day marched through a wood of date trees to attack the enemy on the ridge of heights in front. As the British emerged from among the trees, the French advanced from the high ground and commenced the action. The brigade to which the THIRTEENTH belonged was advancing in column, when it was charged by a body of French cavalry, which was repulsed by the ninetieth regiment, forming the advance-guard of the right column. Major-General Cradock instantly formed the brigade under a heavy fire, and the gallant conduct of the regiments was equal to the most sanguine expectation of their commander. The French were driven from their position, and compelled to retreat over the plains into the lines on the heights before Alexandria.

The regiment had Captain Chester, one serjeant, 1801 and fifteen rank and file killed; Captain Brown, Lieutenant Dolphin, and three soldiers, died of their wounds; Lieutenants Handcock, Copland, Serle, and Rich, Ensigns Hewson, Andrews, and O'Malley, three serjeants, and ninety-seven rank and file, wounded.

In general orders, issued on the following day, it was stated—'The Commander-in-chief has the greatest 'satisfaction in thanking the troops for their soldier- 'like and intrepid conduct in the action of yesterday; 'he feels it incumbent on him particularly to express 'his most perfect satisfaction with the steady and 'gallant conduct of Major-General Cradock's brigade.' This brigade consisted of the eighth, THIRTEENTH, eighteenth, and ninetieth regiments.

The French forces at *Alexandria* having been augmented in numbers by the arrival of additional troops from the interior, General Menou advanced early on the morning of the 21st of March, and attacked the English position with great intrepidity; but the French were repulsed at every point of attack, and the British soldiers stood triumphant over Buonaparte's "*invincible*" legions, at the close of the third engagement on the distant shores of Egypt. Sir Ralph Abercromby was wounded in the action, and died a few days afterwards, much regretted by the army: he was succeeded by Lieut.-General (afterwards Lord) Hutchinson.

After this victory, one division traversed the country to Rosetta, and captured the forts at that place; part of the army then advanced up the river Nile, and forced the French troops at the city of Cairo to surrender. The THIRTEENTH foot were, however, not employed in these services, but were engaged in the *blockade of Alexandria*.

1801 A body of troops arrived in Egypt from India; the forces which had captured Cairo returned to the vicinity of Alexandria, and the siege of this city was commenced. The French were unable to defend the place, and they surrendered in the beginning of September. Egypt was thus delivered from the power of the French "*Army of the East,*" which was forced to quit that country, shorn of its laurels, and to return to France with blighted hopes.

The British soldiers received the thanks of Parliament, and the expression of their Sovereign's approbation of their heroic conduct; and the "SPHINX," with the word "EGYPT," on the colours of the THIRTEENTH REGIMENT, commemorates its gallant conduct on this splendid enterprise. The Grand Seignior established an order of Knighthood, of which the general officers were made members; and large gold medals were presented to the field officers, captains, and subalterns.

As a further proof of the estimation in which the Grand Seignior held the services of the British soldiers in Egypt, he ordered a palace to be built at Constantinople for the future residence of the British Ambassadors.

NAMES of the officers of the THIRTEENTH Regiment who received gold medals for service in Egypt:—

Lieut.-Colonels.	*Majors.*
Lawrence Bradshaw.	Edward Scott (*Lieut.-Colonel*).
Hon. Charles Colville	G. Kinnaird Dana
(*Commanding the regiment.*)	(*Lt.-Colonel*).

Captains.

Francis Weller.	John O'Neil Bayley.
William Belford.	Arthur Wilkinson.
John Beaver Brown (*wounded 13th March*, 1801).	Francis Wm. Schyler.
	John Staunton
A. W. Young.	(*Captain, Lieut. and Captain.*)

REGIMENT OF LIGHT INFANTRY. 51

Lieutenants. 1801

Thomas Serle.	James Blake.
Cæsar Colclough.	James Kearnay Browne.
James Wood.	Richard Huson.
George Innes.	William Trench.
Alexander Patterson.	Patrick Hering.
George Thornhill.	George O'Malley.
Hyacinth Daly.	Eyre Trench.
Richard Butler Handcock (*wounded* 13*th March*, 1801.)	John Dunn.
	Richard M. West.
John Peck (*wounded* 13*th March*, 1801).	

Ensigns.

Soden Davys.	John Richardson.
Brinley Purefoy.	Richard Church.
James Galbreath.	James Fitzsimons O'Reilly.
Edward Sheridan.	John Custice.
Peter Shansey.	

Adjutant, Geo. Parson.—*Quarter-Master*, Edw. Murray.

Surgeon, Wm. Patton.—*Assistant Surgeons*, Jas. McGuire, and Francis Coul.

The British army in Egypt had equalled the most sanguine expectations of their country; and when ages have passed, the story of the gallant achievements of the soldiers who fought under the brave Sir Ralph Abercromby will stimulate to heroic actions the future warriors of the British empire. The English army had proved to the world that French soldiers were not invincible; the expectations of Buonaparte had been defeated, and negociations for a treaty of peace were commenced.

The THIRTEENTH regiment remained in Egypt until 1802 the 13th of January, 1802, when it embarked from Alexandria for the island of Malta, where it arrived on the 2nd of March.

The regiment was stationed at Malta twelve months, during which time a treaty of peace was concluded at

1802 Amiens, on the 25th March, 1802, in which the British government agreed to give up Malta; but the conduct of Buonaparte, then First Consul of France, was marked by so many acts of aggression, that the government considered itself justified in refusing to deliver up the island.

1803 In March, 1803, when hostilities were on the eve of re-commencing, the regiment embarked for Gibraltar, to relieve the second battalion of the royal regiment of foot from garrison duty at that fortress.

1804 On the decease of General Ainslie, in 1804, King George III., conferred the colonelcy of the THIRTEENTH foot on Lieut.-General Sir Alexander Campbell, (who had commanded the seventh West India regiment which was disbanded in 1802,) by commission dated the 11th of July, 1804.

While the regiment was stationed at Gibraltar, a fever of a very fatal character broke out in the town and garrison, and during the months of September, October, and November, the regiment lost four officers, and one hundred and twenty-six non-commissioned officers and private soldiers.

1805 In the autumn of the following year, the regiment was relieved from garrison duty at Gibraltar, and it
1806 landed on the 1st of January, 1806, at Portsmouth, from whence it proceeded to Winchester and Weymouth.

The court of Spain had again united with Napoleon Buonaparte in hostilities against Great Britain, and in August the regiment returned to Portsmouth for the purpose of forming part of an expedition against the Spanish possessions in South America; but the order for the embarkation of the regiment was countermanded, and it marched to Dover, and afterwards to Deal barracks.

REGIMENT OF LIGHT INFANTRY.   53

The regiment left Deal on the 4th of May, 1807, for 1807 Ramsgate, where it embarked for Ireland; and landing at Monkstown on the 23rd of May, marched from thence to Middleton barracks and afterwards to Cahir.

In the autumn, the regiment was completed to its establishment by volunteers from the militia, and embarking at Monkstown for England, landed at Portsmouth on the 2nd of December.

On the 26th of January, 1808, the regiment embarked 1808 for the West Indies, and on its arrival it was appointed to the garrison of Bermuda, where it landed on the 26th of March.

The West India islands belonging to France, which had been restored to that country at the peace of Amiens in 1802, had not been recaptured at the recommencement of hostilities in 1803; but in 1808 an expedition was assembled at Carlisle Bay, Barbadoes, for the reduction of the French island of *Martinique;* the land forces were under Lieut.-General George Beckwith, and the navy was commanded by Rear-Admiral Sir Alexander Cochrane, K.B. The THIRTEENTH foot embarked from Bermuda on the 23rd of November to join the expedition, and remained at Barbadoes until the armament was ready for the enterprise.

The fleet left Carlisle Bay on the 28th of January, 1809 1809, and arrived off the island of *Martinique* in two days. On the 30th, the troops landed in two divisions; the first division at Bay Robert, under Lieut.-General Sir George Prevost; and the second division, commanded by Major-General Maitland, near St. Luce and Point Solomon. Both divisions were actively engaged in operations for the reduction of the island. After a night march of seven miles through a difficult country, the first division occupied a position on the Great Lizard

1809 River; and on the 1st of February it engaged the enemy on Morne Brune and the heights of Surirey, which were warmly contested; but British valour was triumphant. In eight days from the time the fleet quitted Barbadoes, Fort Desaix (or Fort Bourbon) was invested, 'notwithstanding heavy rains, 'and most unfavourable weather, in which the troops 'have borne every species of privation in a manner 'worthy the character of British soldiers.'* The siege of the fort was prosecuted with vigour; and on the 24th February, the French governor, General Villaret, surrendered, the French twenty-sixth and eighty-second regiments becoming prisoners, and delivering up their arms and EAGLES to the British troops. The conduct of the regiment, at the capture of this valuable island, was afterwards rewarded with the royal authority to bear on its colours the word "MARTINIQUE," to commemorate its services on this occasion.

The THIRTEENTH were stationed at Martinique, where they received two hundred and fifty volunteers from the English militia, in October, 1809.

1810 A strong detachment of the regiment embarked from Martinique on the 21st of January, 1810, and sailed to Prince Rupert's, Dominica, where it joined the expedition against *Guadaloupe*, under the orders of Lieut.-General Beckwith: the detachment of the THIRTEENTH, sixty-third (600 rank and file), York light infantry volunteers, and fourth West India regiment, formed the fourth brigade under Brigadier-General Skinner, in the first division, commanded by Major-General Hislop. This division sailed from Dominica on the 26th of January, landed at St. Mary's, in Capesterre, on the 28th, and took an active part in the operations by which the French troops in the island of Guada-

* Lieut.-General Beckwith's despatch.

REGIMENT OF LIGHT INFANTRY. 55

loupe were forced to surrender on the 6th of February. 1810
The loss of the THIRTEENTH foot, in this service, was
limited to one man killed and five wounded; and immediately after the capture of the island, the detachment rejoined the regiment at Martinique.

During the years 1811 and 1812, the THIRTEENTH 1811
were stationed at the island of Martinique. 1812

On the 15th of February, 1813, General Campbell 1813
was removed to the thirty-second regiment, and was
succeeded in the colonelcy of the THIRTEENTH by
Lieut.-General Edward Morrison, from Colonel-Commandant in the sixtieth foot.

In the meantime, the measures adopted by the
English government, to counteract the tyrannical decrees
of Napoleon, designed for the destruction of the
commerce of Great Britain, had involved England in
war with the United States of America, and the frontiers of Canada had become the theatre of conflict, to
which the THIRTEENTH foot were directed to repair.
The regiment accordingly embarked from Fort Royal,
Martinique, on the 2nd of May, 1813, arrived on the
28th of June at Quebec, and proceeded from thence in
steam-boats and bateaux to Montreal.

At this period, a numerous American force had
penetrated Upper Canada; and a small expedition was
fitted out on Lake Champlain, with the view of calling
the attention of the Americans to the defence of their
own settlements on the borders of that sheet of water.
To engage in this service, nine officers and one hundred
and eighty-one soldiers of the THIRTEENTH foot crossed
the river St. Lawrence in boats, on the 24th and 25th
of July, and proceeded to the Isle aux Noix, where an
expedition was assembled under Lieut.-Colonel J.
Murray; Lieut.-Colonel William Williams, of the
THIRTEENTH, being second in command. Sailing from

1813 the Isle aux Noix in boats, the expedition navigated the lake, and as it approached the enemy's post at *Plattsburg*, the American militia abandoned the place. The British landed, destroyed the arsenal, block-house, commissary's buildings and stores, with the barracks at Saranac, capable of containing four thousand men. The flotilla afterwards returned to Isle aux Noix. In concluding his public despatch, Lieut.-Colonel Murray expressed his sense of the conduct of Lieut.-Colonel Williams, of the THIRTEENTH foot, in terms of commendation; and added, 'I have to report in the highest 'terms of approbation, the discipline, regularity, and 'cheerful conduct of the whole of the troops; and feel 'fully confident, that, had an opportunity offered, their 'courage would have been equally conspicuous.'

1814 Active operations were continued during the winter, when the weather permitted; and in the spring of 1814, Lieut.-Colonel Williams, of the THIRTEENTH foot, had charge of the advance-posts on the river Richelieu.

The American commander, Major-General Wilkinson, concentrated a considerable force for the invasion of Lower Canada; the THIRTEENTH and forty-ninth regiments, the Canadian voltigeurs, a troop of the nineteenth light dragoons, and a field train, were assembled at St. John's, and its vicinity, to oppose the invaders. This force was placed under the orders of Colonel Sir Sidney Beckwith, and it was ordered to dislodge a body of Americans, who had taken post at Philipsburg, in the seigniory of St. Armand; but the enemy made a precipitate retreat across the ice on Lake Champlain.

On the 30th of March, the American light troops entered Odell-town, followed by three brigades of infantry, a squadron of cavalry, and eleven guns; they drove in the British piquets, and attacked the post at Burton Ville; but were so well received by the troops stationed there, that they soon desisted in the attempt on that post. Their leading brigades afterwards attacked the mill and block-house on the *La Cole* river, where a detachment of the THIRTEENTH foot and a party of Canadians were stationed, under Major Handcock, of the THIRTEENTH. The Americans drove in the piquet, gained possession of a wood, established a battery among the trees, and opened a sharp fire upon the post, which was gallantly defended. Major Handcock having ascertained that the flank companies of the THIRTEENTH had arrived at the mill, directed an effort to be made to capture the American artillery, when Captain Ellard led his company to the charge with distinguished bravery, and a spirited attempt was made on the battery; but the wood was found crowded with American infantry. Captain Ellard was severely wounded, and the few men who had made the sally, finding themselves opposed by several entire regiments of the enemy, withdrew from the unequal contest. The Americans persevering in the attack, a second attempt was made to capture their guns, but their brigades were too numerous to admit of a chance of success. The post was, however, successfully defended; every attempt of the Americans to capture it was repelled, and they retired, after sustaining considerable loss.

Major Handcock, and the officers and soldiers who had so nobly defended this post, were thanked for their conduct, by the commander of the forces, Lieut.-General Sir George Prevost. The regiment had thirteen rank and file killed; Captain Ellard, Ensign Whitford, two serjeants, and forty-six rank and file wounded.

1814   In April the war with France was terminated, and Napoleon Buonaparte was removed from the throne of that kingdom; but the contest in America was continued, and the THIRTEENTH regiment was employed on the frontiers of Lower Canada, but it had no opportunity of distinguishing itself.

1815   Peace was concluded with the United States in 1815, when the regiment received orders to return to England: it embarked from the Isle aux Noix in bateaux, was removed into smaller boats at William Henry, on the river St. Lawrence, and embarking in transports at the Three Rivers, arrived at Portsmouth on the 15th of July, when it landed, and was employed in garrison duty at that fortress. The period of its arrival from America, did not, therefore, afford an opportunity of the services of the regiment being available on the occasion of the return of Buonaparte to France, his overthrow at Waterloo, nor on the restoration of Louis XVIII.

The regiment remained at Portsmouth until August, when it embarked for the island of Jersey, where it was stationed upwards of two years; and its orderly conduct, on all occasions, procured for it the respect and esteem of the inhabitants and civil authorities of the island.

1816   In January, 1816, an order was received for the reduction of the regiment to ten companies, of sixty rank and file each.

1817   On the 24th of May, 1817, new colours were presented to the regiment, on the parade in Fort Regent-square, Jersey. The colours bore on them the "SPHINX," with the words "EGYPT" and "MARTINIQUE," and were consecrated by the Rev. George Lawrence, garrison chaplain, who delivered a very learned and suitable address to the regiment on the occasion.

In June of the same year, the establishment was

augmented to nine hundred and seven officers and 1817 soldiers.

The regiment embarked from Jersey in August, and proceeded to the islands of Guernsey and Alderney. Its conduct, while at Jersey, had excited the admiration of the inhabitants and civil authorities of the island; and on its departure, a numerous public meeting of the inhabitants and functionaries of the parish of Saint Heliers, expressed the high sense they entertained of the distinguished merits of the corps, which was communicated to the commanding officer, Colonel Sir William Williams, by the principal constable of St. Helier. The states of the island also passed an act, setting forth their estimation of the discipline and orderly behaviour of the regiment;* which was communi-

---

* 'Aux Etats de l'île de Jersey. L'an mil huit cent dix-sept, le vingtième
'jour d'Août.—Sensibles aux soins que le Lieutenant-Colonel Messire
'William Williams, et tous les autres officiers du treizième régiment d'in-
'fanterie de Sa Majesté, ont apporté durant leur séjour dans ce pays à ce
'concilier l'estime des habitans, et à y entretenir une heureuse harmonie,
'et pleinement satisfaits du haut dégré de discipline dans lequel ils ont
'constamment gardé et maintenu le dit régiment, et leur attention à prevenir
'tout sujets de plaintes et de disputes, à faire observer l'ordre et respecter
'les lois, du zèle avec lequel ils se sont toujours prêtés à soutenir et à
'appuyer les autorités constituées, Les Etats saisissent cette occasion de
'leur première séance depuis que le dit régiment a été rapellé hors du ser-
'vice de cette île, où il a été en quartier pendant deux ans, pour leur
'rendre par ce présente acte, le témoignage de leur approbation et leur
'exprimer leur vive reconnaissance. Et les Etats prient le Lieutenant-
'Colonel Messire William Williams, Chevalier commandeur de l'honor-
'able ordre du Bain, le Lieutenant-Colonel Weller, et le Lieutenant-
'Colonel Hancock, qui ont chacun d'eux, l'un après l'autre, eu le com-
'mandement du dit régiment, et tous les autres officiers de ce corps, d'en
'accepter leurs sincères et unanimes remerciments. Les Etats ont requis Son
'Excellence Monsieur le lieutenant-gouverneur de vouloir bien transmettre,
'de leur part, le présent acte, au lieutenant-colonel Messire William Wil-
'liams, lequel est prié de le communiquer à Lieutenant-Colonel Weller,
'au Lieutenant-Colonel Hancock, et à tous les autres officiers du treizième
'régiment, auquel effet le greffier est chargé de le transcrire sur parchemin,
'afin qu'il soit mis sous le sçeau de l'île et de le remettre à Son Excellence.'

FRS. GODFRAY, Greffier.

1817 cated to the commanding officer, by his Excellency Major-General H. M. Gordon. In acknowledging the receipt of the act of the states, Colonel Sir William Williams observed, 'To possess the good wishes of 'those with whom a soldier resides must ever be the 'most pleasing reflection, but particularly where, in the 'performance of his duty, approval emanates from so 'high and so respectable an assembly as the states of 'Jersey; it thence becomes a source of the most heart-'felt and lasting gratification, and will be recorded, and 'handed down, as one of their dearest memorials. In 'communicating the contents to the officers of the 'THIRTEENTH regiment, I am to request you may ac-'cept their thanks; they being actuated with the most 'fervent wishes for the prosperity of the island.'

1818 The regiment remained at the islands of Guernsey and Alderney during the two following years. In October, 1818, the establishment was reduced to seven hundred and forty-six officers and soldiers. In May 1819 and June, 1819, the regiment embarked by detachments for Portsmouth.

On quitting Guernsey, the following letter was received, dated 4th May, 1819:—

'SIR,
'The Royal Court of this island have desired 'me, as their president, to express the high regard 'which they in common with its inhabitants entertain 'for the officers of His Majesty's THIRTEENTH regi-'ment of foot; as well as their approbation and ad-'miration of the general good conduct of the men of 'that corps, while quartered among us; and I feel 'much pleasure, in being thus enabled to assure you, 'Sir, that from all classes I have heard no other senti-

'ments but those of regret, at the approaching depart- 1819
'ure of the THIRTEENTH regiment, which under your
'command, and that of Lieut.-Col. Sir William Wil-
'liams, has shown itself throughout so orderly, and
'worthy of the esteem of this and the neighbouring
'islands; and the officers in particular, by their gentle-
'manly and social manners, have so thoroughly gained
'the good will of those who had the pleasure of their
'acquaintance, that one and all unite in the best
'wishes for the happiness and prosperity of the whole
'corps, in which none is more sincere than he who has
'the honour to be,

'Sir, yours, &c.,
'PETER DE HAVILLAND,
'Bailiff of Guernsey.'

In acknowledging the receipt of this letter, Lieut.-Colonel R. B. Hancock, stated,—' It will, no doubt,
'be extremely gratifying to Sir William Williams, as it
'is to all ranks of the regiment now here, to find that
'their conduct has been thought deserving of so great
'an honour. Penetrated by the repeated proofs of
'esteem and affection, which they have received from
'the inhabitants of Guernsey, the officers request me
'to offer their sincere wishes for the general prosperity
'of the island, and for the individual happiness and
'welfare of those friends to whose polite and marked
'attention they are so deeply indebted.'

In September the regiment embarked for Scotland, and landing at Leith, proceeded from thence to Stirling castle, with detachments to Dumbarton castle, Paisley, Callender, and Buchlivie.

The regiment marched to Edinburgh castle in Sep- 1820
tember, 1820: towards the end of October it proceeded

1820 to Port Patrick, where it embarked for Ireland, landing at Donaghadee, marched from thence to Dublin, with detachments to Stranorlane, Carndonagh, Green-castle, Buncrana, Rethinilton, and Letterkenny.

1821 After occupying these stations ten months, the regiment called in its detachments, and marched to Richmond barracks, Dublin, where it arrived on the 21st of September, 1821.

1822 From Dublin the regiment embarked, on the 18th of July, 1822, for England, and two days after landing at Liverpool, orders were received from the Horse Guards for the regiment to embark for Greenock, proceed from thence to Edinburgh, and do duty there during the visit of His Majesty King George IV. to that city.

The regiment arrived at Edinburgh on the 31st of July and 1st of August: it had the honour of mounting guard over the royal person, when the King visited that city, and Captain Ellard, who commanded the guard of honor assembled to receive His Majesty on landing, obtained the brevet rank of major.

After His Majesty's departure, the regiment embarked for Chatham, where it arrived on the 21st, 23rd, and 24th of September.

The regiment having been selected to proceed to India, made preparations for transferring its services to that part of the British dominions. Previous to embarking, it was constituted a corps of LIGHT INFANTRY, to take date as such from the 25th of December, 1822; and the usual augmentation was made to its numbers.

1823 On the 1st and 3rd of January, 1823, the regiment embarked on board the 'General Kydd' and 'Kent' Indiamen, under Lieut.-Col. Mc. Creagh and Major

THIRTEENTH,
PRINCE ALBERT'S REGIMENT OF
LIGHT INFANTRY.

Robert H. Sale, and landed in May at Calcutta, where 1823 it received six hundred and twenty volunteers from corps about to return to England.

Soon after the arrival of the regiment in India, the 1824 tranquillity of the eastern dominions of Great Britain was interrupted by the sovereign of Ava, who governed a numerous nation of Burmans, inhabiting an extensive territory, lying in one direction, between the Chinese dominions and Bengal. For many years the Burmese officers, in the country contiguous to the British territory, had been guilty of acts of encroachment and aggression, which at length became of so outrageous a character, as to render it necessary to call upon the court of Ava for an explanation. No answer was given; but after overcoming several petty tribes by which his kingdom was surrounded, the King of Ava made preparations for invading the British territory. Troops were assembled to penetrate the Burman empire, and to put an end to these acts of aggression; and an armament was prepared at Port Cornwallis, under the command of Brigadier-General Sir Archibald Campbell and Commodore Grant, for the capture of *Rangoon*, a city, and the principal part of the Burmese empire, situate on the north bank of the river Irawaddy, thirty miles from the sea. The THIRTEENTH light infantry embarked on this service, on the 5th of April, 1824; their commanding officer, Lieut.-Colonel Mc. CREAGH was appointed to the command of a brigade, with the rank of Brigadier-General, and the command of the regiment devolved on Major SALE. The fleet entered the Irawaddy on the 10th of May: the Burmese made a feeble attempt to defend the city, but their batteries were soon silenced, and the place was captured without the loss of a man; the inhabitants

1824 quitting their houses and seeking refuge in the thickly-wooded country.

Brigadier-General Mc. Creagh was detached with three companies against the island of *Cheduba*, on the Arracan coast, where he landed on the 14th of May, captured the Burmese stockade by storm on the 17th, made the rajah, or governor, prisoner, and reduced this fertile and productive island to submission: in which service the THIRTEENTH had Brevet Major Thornhill, Ensign Kershaw, one serjeant, one bugler, and eighteen rank and file wounded.

The Burmese army continued in great force in the neighbourhood of Rangoon, under the protection of fortifications of wood, called stockades, and of the thick jungle which covered the face of the country.

On the 28th of May, a hundred rank and file of the THIRTEENTH regiment, commanded by Major William H. Dennie, with a detachment of the thirty-eighth, advanced, under Sir Archibald Campbell, and attacked two stockades by storm, without ladders, captured the works with the bayonet, and killed about five hundred of the enemy. The THIRTEENTH had Lieutenant A. Howard killed; one bugler, and nine rank and file wounded.

When driven from one series of stockades, the Burmese erected another at a greater distance. On the 10th of June, two companies of the THIRTEENTH, under Major Robert Henry Sale, advanced with other troops, to attack the enemy's stronghold at *Kemmendine;* when about two miles from the town, the head of the column was stopped by a strong stockade, full of men, against which the British artillery opened a well-directed fire, and in half an hour a breach was made. The forty-first, and part of the Madras European regiment, stormed

the works in front; and the detachments of the Thir- 1824
teenth and thirty eighth assaulted the rear face
which was ten feet high. The soldiers being encouraged and animated by the spirited conduct of Major
Sale, who showed an example of valour and personal
agility, climbed the works, one helping another up, and
entering simultaneously with the party by the breach,
they bayoneted every man that opposed them. The
loss of the Thirteenth was limited to one private
soldier killed; Lieutenant Petry, and ten soldiers
wounded.*

This point being gained, the column advanced about
a mile, and at four o'clock in the afternoon, took up a
position against the enemy's principal stockade: batteries were erected during the night, the artillery
opened a heavy fire at daylight, and the Burmese for-
sook their works and fled.

On the 17th of June, Brigadier-General M'Creagh
joined with the three companies from the island of
Cheduba.

In the beginning of July numerous columns of
Burmese warriors were seen in front of the British
position, when four companies were ordered to make a
reconnoissance under the command of Major Dennie:
they discovered the enemy in force on the plains of
Kumaroot, and returned with the loss of one man
wounded. On the same day, the Burmese attacked

---

* 'A very spirited and successful attack was made on the other side of
'the stockade, by the advance companies of the Thirteenth and thirty-
'eighth regiments, under the command of Major Sale, who, by assisting each
'other up the face of the stockade, at least ten feet high, entered about the
'same time as the party by the breach, putting every man to death who
'opposed their entrance : and it affords me pleasure to state, that the first
'man who appeared on the top of the work was, I believe, Major Sale of
'His Majesty's Thirteenth Light Infantry.'—*Major-General Sir A.
Campbell's Despatch.*

1824 the British posts, but were repulsed: the THIRTEENTH had two men wounded.

The Burmese position in the rear of the great pagoda was attacked on the 5th of July, when the regiment had one private soldier killed; Lieutenant Knox Barrett, one serjeant, and sixteen rank and file wounded.

A general attack was made on the 8th of July, and three hundred men of the THIRTEENTH, under Brigadier-General M'Creagh, formed part of the force detached, under Brigadier-General M'Bean, to storm the enemy's works. The attack was led by Major Sale, at the head of the soldiers of the THIRTEENTH regiment, with heroic gallantry, and seven stockades were carried in rapid succession. Major Sale encountered the Burmese commander-in-chief in the works, and slew him in single combat, taking from him a valuable gold-hilted sword and scabbard. Three other stockades were captured by other portions of the armament; and the men, under Brigadier-General M'Bean, fell in with a number of Burmese flying from a stockade attacked by the shipping, of whom they bayoneted a great number. Eight hundred Burmese were killed on this occasion, and thirty-eight pieces of artillery, forty swivels, and three hundred muskets were captured.*

Two serjeants of the THIRTEENTH were killed;

* 'Nothing could have been more brilliant and successful. He (Brigadier-General M'Bean) took by assault seven stockades with most rapid succession, throwing the enemy into the utmost consternation.' . . . . . . 'The brigadier-general assures me the ardour of his column was irresistible, and speaks highly of the able aid he received from Brigadier-General M'Creagh; he also reports favourably upon the judicious and gallant style in which Majors Sale and Frith, of the THIRTEENTH and thirty-eighth regiments, led the troops under their respective command.'—*Major-General Sir A. Campbell's Despatch.*

Captain Johnson, two corporals, and five private soldiers were wounded.

The terror of these attacks caused the Burmese troops to remove to a greater distance; and the difficult character of the country, rainy weather, inundations, and the necessity for procuring a large supply of provisions before the army advanced, detained the British some time in the neighbourhood of Rangoon.

Meanwhile the Burmese recovered from the consternation into which they had been thrown, and a veteran chief, named Maha Bandoola, was appointed commander of the army of Ava. This chief approached the British position on the 1st of December, with upwards of fifty thousand foot, a body of Cassay horse, and three hundred pieces of artillery, and commenced forming entrenchments. The British beheld the legions of Ava, ten times more numerous than themselves, without dismay; and the left of the Burmese line presenting a favourable opportunity for an attack, Major Sale advanced with two hundred of the THIRTEENTH Light Infantry, under Major Dennie, and two hundred and fifty of the eighteenth Native Infantry, under Captain Ross, and stormed the entrenchments with distinguished gallantry, in sight of the whole army. The soldiers of the THIRTEENTH led the charge with great intrepidity; they burst through the entrenchments, overthrew all opposition, and spread terror and dismay on the enemy's flank. The native infantry followed the example; the Burmese fled, and the victorious British soldiers returned to their posts laden with trophies.*

* ' I never witnessed a more dashing charge than was made on this occa-
' sion by His Majesty's THIRTEENTH Light Infantry; while the eighteenth
' native infantry followed their example with a spirit that did them honour,

1824 The THIRTEENTH foot had Lieutenant O'Shea, one serjeant, and three rank and file killed; Captain Clark died of his wounds: Ensigns Blackwall and Croker, one serjeant, and twenty rank and file wounded.

This victory was followed by a decisive triumph over the left wing of the Burmese army, on the 5th of December, on which occasion two hundred and forty-five rank and file of the THIRTEENTH, under Major Dennie, formed part of the first column of attack, under Major Sale, which penetrated the enemy's lines, and routed the legions of Ava with a facility which proved the superior prowess of British soldiers. The first advantage was followed up, the powerful army of the enemy was overthrown, and of the three hundred pieces of ordnance which the enemy had in position, two hundred and forty were brought into the British camp.* The loss of the regiment was six rank and file wounded.

Anxious to retrieve his disgrace, the Burmese commander rallied his broken legions, called reinforcements to his aid, and took up another position, which he fortified with great labour and art. These formidable works were attacked on the 15th of December, when two hundred of the THIRTEENTH, under

' carrying all opposition before them. They burst through the entrench-
' ments, carrying dismay and terror into the enemy's ranks, great numbers
' of whom were slain, and the party returned loaded with arms, standards,
' and other trophies.'—*Major-General Sir A. Campbell's Despatch.*

* ' All their artillery, stores, and reserve depôts, which had cost them so
' much labour to get up, with a great quantity of small arms, gilt chattahs,
' standards, and other trophies fell into our hands. Never was victory more
' complete or decided, and never was a triumph of discipline and valour, over
' the disjointed efforts of irregular courage and infinitely superior numbers,
' more conspicuous. Majors Dennie and Thornhill, of the THIRTEENTH
' Light Infantry were distinguished by the steadiness with which they led
' their men.'—*Major-General Sir A. Campbell's Despatch.*

Major Sale, formed part of the column of attack under
Brigadier-General Cotton, which made a detour round
the enemy's left to gain the rear of his position at
Kokien, which was to be attacked in front by another
column. On arriving in front of the position it
presented a very formidable appearance; but the
English general knew from experience the character of
the troops he commanded, and he gave the signal for
the attack, when the soldiers rushed forward with the
most determined and enthusiastic bravery, and in less
than fifteen minutes they were in full possession of
these stupendous works. The THIRTEENTH met with
very determined resistance; their commanding officer,
Major Sale, received a severe wound in the head; he
was succeeded by Major Dennie, who was wounded in
the hand, but who continued at the head of the
regiment until the action was over. The Burmese
only resisted a short time, and then fled in a panic,
leaving their camp standing, all their baggage, and a
great portion of their arms and ammunition behind
them.

Lieutenants Darby, Petry, and Jones, two serjeants,
and seven rank and file, of the THIRTEENTH, were
killed; Majors Sale * and Dennie, Captains Thornhill
(Brevet Major) and James M'Pherson, Lieutenants
M. Fenton and Pattisson, Ensigns Wilkinson and
Blackwell, two serjeants, and forty rank and file
wounded.

These splendid successes, connected with the services

* ' In the list of wounded will be seen with regret the name of Major
' SALE of His Majesty's THIRTEENTH Light Infantry, an officer whose
' gallantry has been most conspicuous on every occasion since our arrival at
' Rangoon. I am happy to say that his wound, though severe, is not dan-
' gerous, and I trust his valuable services will not long remain unavail-
' able.'--*Major-General Sir A. Campbell's Despatch.*

1824 of the royal navy, had produced important results; the maritime provinces of Mergui, Tavoy, Yeb, and Martuban, had been captured, and seven hundred pieces of artillery had been taken from the Burmese. To wrest additional territory from the court of Ava, the THIRTEENTH regiment was detached, under Major Dennie, with other troops, the whole under Major Sale, against the city of *Bassein*, in the south-west part of the ancient kingdom of Pegu, which constituted part of the Burmese empire. The regiment
1825 embarked on this service on the 10th of February, and after a tedious passage arrived, on the evening of the 14th, off Pagoda Point, Great Negrais. On the 26th the expedition entered the river, and the THIRTEENTH, thirty-eighth, and twelfth Native Infantry landed and captured a stockade. The troops afterwards re-embarked, and proceeded to the next stockade, which the Burmese abandoned as the soldiers went on shore to storm the works; and so great was the consternation of the enemy, that the city of Bassein was set on fire and abandoned. The expedition anchored opposite the smoking ruins on the 3rd of March, when the troops landed and took post in the area of the principal pagoda: many private houses were not destroyed, and the inhabitants were induced to return to their homes. On the 13th of March, Major Dennie made a reconnoissance up the Bassein river; he was afterwards joined by another party under Major Sale, and the whole proceeded one hundred and twenty miles up the river, to Lanrince, and returned to Bassein on the 23rd, having had two men wounded.

No resistance being met with in the province of Bassein, the THIRTEENTH regiment embarked for Rangoon, where it arrived on the 2nd of May; mean-

while the army under Lieut.-General Sir Archibald 1825
Campbell had advanced up the country, and had captured several strong towns.

On the 8th of August, the regiment embarked from Rangoon, to join the army at Prome, where it arrived in boats on the 25th. Soon afterwards overtures of peace were made by the Burmese, but hostilities were resumed in the middle of November; and the army of Ava having repulsed the attack of three bodies of sepoys, became suddenly elevated with a high idea of its own power, and advanced to envelop the British troops at Prome.

About sixty thousand Burmese environed six thousand British and native Indian troops; but undismayed by this formidable host, the English general left four native regiments for the defence of Prome, and advanced, on the 1st of December, to attack the enemy's left wing at *Simbike*. This post was stormed by the troops under Brigadier-General Cotton,* and the works were carried, in gallant style, in ten minutes. The THIRTEENTH were engaged in the operation, but did not take part in the assault.

After a harassing march of about twenty miles, the troops bivouacked at Ze-ouke, and at daylight on the following morning (2nd December) they were again in motion, to attack the formidable position occupied by the enemy's centre division on the *Napadee Hills*. Arriving in the vicinity of the position, the British artillery commenced a sharp cannonade; Brigadier-General Elrington's troops drove the enemy from the jungle, six companies of the eighty-seventh regiment carried the posts at the

* Now Lieut.-General Sir Willoughby Cotton, Commanding the Forces at Bombay.

1825 bottom of the ridge, and the Burmese were driven from the valley to their principal works on the hills, which appeared very formidable; the heights could only be ascended by a narrow road, commanded by artillery, and defended by stockades crowded with men armed with muskets. As soon as the artillery had made an impression on the works, the THIRTEENTH and thirty-eighth regiments sprang forward with astonishing resolution and steadiness, rushed into the enemy's works, overthrowing all opposition with the bayonet, and driving the Burmese from hill to hill, over precipices that could only be ascended by a narrow stair, until the whole of the position, nearly three miles in length, was captured. Lieut.-Colonel Sale and Major Thornhill, of the THIRTEENTH regiment, distinguished themselves.

On the 5th of December, the enemy's right wing was driven from its post; the immense army of Ava was thus forced from its positions by the fierce attacks of the British soldiers; and the Burmese legions sought safety in flight.

After this success, the army continued to advance; the Burmese evacuated Meeday, and took post at *Melloon*, at the same time they renewed their offers for terminating the war; but this appears to have been done with the view of gaining time to re-organize their army for a more determined resistance.

1826 The conditions of peace not being ratified by the stipulated time, hostilities were resumed on the 19th of January, 1826, on which day the THIRTEENTH and Thirty-eighth regiments embarked in boats under Lieut.-Colonel Sale, to assault the main face of the enemy's fortifications at Melloon; at the same time other corps embarked to storm the works at different points. The whole of the boats quitted the shore together; but the current and breeze carried the THIRTEENTH and thirty-eighth to their point of attack, before the other divisions could reach the opposite bank of the river, and Lieut.-Colonel Sale was wounded in his boat; but the two regiments landed, formed under the command of Major Frith of the thirty-eighth, and rushed forward with such intrepidity and resolution, that they overpowered all resistance, and were speedily masters of these formidable works.* Major Frith was wounded in the assault, and the command of the brigade devolved on Major THORNHILL, of the THIRTEENTH regiment, who distinguished himself.

1826

The loss of the regiment was one man killed; Major Sale and three men wounded.

The army advanced upon the capital of the Burmese empire, and the legions of Ava resolved once more to try their fortune in battle; they met the British in the open fields near *Pagahm Mew*, where an action took place on the 9th of February. The THIRTEENTH led the right attack in their usual gallant style, the Burmese troops soon gave way before the superior prowess of the British soldiers, and another victory was gained. The regiment had one soldier killed; Captain Tronson and six soldiers wounded.

After this victory, the army continued its advance upon Ummerapoora, the capital, situated upon the shores of a romantic lake; and when within four days march of that city, the King of Ava sent the ratified treaty, paying the expenses of the war and giving up a considerable portion of territory.

---

* 'The conduct of His Majesty's THIRTEENTH and thirty-eighth regi-
' ments, during the advance, and their gallantry in the storm, far exceed
' all that I can write in their praise.'--*Major-General Sir A. Campbell's
Despatch.*

1826 On the conclusion of this splendid undertaking, the following statement appeared in orders:—' While the 'Governor General in Council enumerates, with senti-'ments of unfeigned admiration, the achievements of 'the first, or royals, the 13th, 38th, 41st, 45th, 47th, '87th, and 89th regiments, the Honorable Company's 'Madras European regiment, and the Bengal and 'Madras European artillery, as the European troops 'which have had the honour of establishing the 'renown of the British arms in a new and distant 'region, His Lordship in Council feels that higher 'and more justly-merited praise cannot be bestowed 'on those brave troops than that, amidst the bar-'barous hosts with which they have fought and con-'quered, they have eminently displayed the virtues, 'and sustained the character of the British Soldier.'

Lieut.-Colonel SALE, and Majors DENNIE and THORNHILL, were rewarded with the honour of being constituted Companions of the Bath: and the word "AVA," on the colours of the regiment, commemorates its gallantry during these campaigns.

The regiment embarked in boats, from Yandaboo, on the 7th of March, arrived at Rangoon on the 22nd, proceeded on board of transports on the 23rd, and arrived at Calcutta in the middle of April.

After remaining a few days at Calcutta, the regiment embarked by divisions for Berhampore, where it was stationed several months.

On the 15th of November, the regiment commenced its march from Berhampore, for Dinapore, where it 1827 arrived on the 3rd of January, 1827.

The regiment remained at Dinapore nearly five 1831 years, and towards the end of 1831, commenced its march for Agra, a city situate on the river Jumnah, the capital of a province of the same name, where it arrived in January, 1832. 1832

At the city of Agra, which exhibits numerous marks of its ancient greatness, the regiment was stationed four years. From Agra the regiment marched, in December, 1835, for Kurnaul, where it arrived in January, 1836. 1835 1836

Early in the year 1837, the regiment furnished a detachment, under the command of Captain N. Chadwick, to accompany the commander-in-chief, General Sir Henry Fane, G.C.B, on a visit to the ruler of the Sikhs, Maharajah Runjeet Singh, at Lahore, the capital of his dominions. After a journey of several weeks, General Sir Henry Fane arrived at Lahore on the 10th of March, and was greeted at the court of the ruler of the Sikhs by a gorgeous display of oriental magnificence, for which Asiatic potentates have been celebrated. The British troops which accompanied the commander-in-chief, were reviewed, on the 17th of March, by the Maharajah, who expressed great admiration of their appearance and discipline, and in a general order published immediately after the review, it was stated, 1837

The Commander-in-Chief has much pleasure in
' communicating to the officers, non-commissioned
' officers, and soldiers of the escort, that their appear-
' ance and steadiness under arms, this morning, met with
' much approbation, and their performance of the vari-
' ous movements will leave in the Punjaub a very
' favourable impression of their discipline.'

Very valuable presents were made to the officers of the escort, and the Maharajah also gave eleven thousand rupees (1100*l.*) to be distributed among the non-commissioned officers and soldiers.

The Commander-in-Chief remained seven weeks at

1837 the capital of the ruler of the Sikhs, and afterwards commenced his journey back to the British dominions, and the officers and soldiers of the THIRTEENTH Light Infantry rejoined the regiment at Kurnaul.

1838 Events occurred in the years 1837 and 1838, which appeared to render a temporary departure from those pacific councils, which have marked the British policy in India, necessary, and which occasioned the THIRTEENTH Light Infantry to take the field, under the following circumstances. Shah Shoojah-ool-Moolk had been driven from the throne of Affghanistan, and his kingdom divided among several chiefs. A Persian army besieged Herat, on the frontiers of Affghanistan, and the court of Persia claimed an extensive portion of that kingdom, which lying between India and Persia appeared to menace the safety of the British dominions in the East Indies. These circumstances, and the unprovoked attack made on an ancient British ally, Runject Singh, by Dost Mahomed Khan, who relied on Persian encouragement and assistance, were followed by the conclusion of a tripartite treaty, between the British, Runjeet Singh, and Shah Shoojah, for the purpose of effecting the restoration of the dethroned monarch of Affghanistan, and a British force was assembled to achieve this important change in the aspect of affairs beyond the river Indus; this force was called the "ARMY OF THE INDUS," and the THIRTEENTH Light Infantry having been selected to take part in this enterprise, left Kurnaul in November, and proceeded to the rendezvous of the army at Ferozepore, where they arrived before the end of the month. They encamped within four miles of the Gharra, beyond which river the crimson tents and pavilions of the army of the Punjaub, designed to co-operate in the enterprise, presented a splendid and imposing appearance. The 1838 ruler of the Sikhs was with his forces; the governor general arrived at the camp, and grand interviews, entertainments, and reviews, took place, which were conducted with great magnificence. In the meantime the Persians had raised the siege of Herat, and the strength of the army was, in consequence thereof, reduced.

From the gala scenes on the banks of the Gharra the troops were called to the more arduous duties of the field, and they advanced upon the capital of the Daoodpootra state; the country was open, the roads good, the air clear and healthful, the river contiguous, and this pleasant march was completed before the end of December, 1838, when the army pitched its tents at the city of Bhawalpore.*

After a short halt, the THIRTEENTH resumed their 1839 march in the beginning of January, 1839, and after passing the boundary of Bhawul Khan, they entered the territory of the Khyrpore Ameer, where the in-

---

* Names of the officers of the THIRTEENTH Light Infantry, who served in the campaign in Affghanistan in 1839.

Lieut.-Colonel's. R. H. Sale, (col.) commanding a brigade.
    ,,   W. H. Dennie   ,,

Major. E. F. Tronson, commanding the regiment.

Captains. G. Fothergill, W. Sutherland, J. Kershaw, R. Pattisson, J. G. D. Taylor, H. N. Vigors.

Lieutenants. A. P. S. Wilkinson, J. H. Fenwick, J. Foulstone, P. R. Jennings, P. D. O. V. Streng, A. E. F. Holcombe, G. King, R. G. Burslem, F. Holder, W. A. Sinclair, Hon. E. J. W. Forester, T. Oxley, D Rattray.

Ensigns. E. King, G. Mein, R. E. Frere.

Paymaster. H. Carew, *Adjutant* H. C. Wade.

Assistant Surgeons J. Robertson, G. W. Barnes.

Captains. T. C. Squire, major of brigade, H. Havelock, aide-de-camp to Major-General Sir Willoughby Cotton, commanding the right division of the army of the Indus.

Lieutenant. J. S. Wood, aide-de-camp to Brigadier General Sale.

Ensign. G. Wade, aide-de-camp to Brigadier-General Dennie.

1839 habitants evinced a disposition bordering on hostility, and withheld aid of every kind. Towards the end of January they arrived at Roree, and beheld the river Indus, which they were about to pass, upwards of half a mile broad, with its banks clothed with groves of date trees covering hills, which presented a striking contrast to the plains near them, green with corn and tamarisk bushes. After some delay, the fortress of Bakkur was delivered up to the British, as a place of arms during the war in Affghanistan.

The troops from Bombay having met with some interruption in their advance through Lower Scinde, part of the Bengal force, including the THIRTEENTH, quitted the Indus, to menace the city of Hyderabad; but returned to Roree in the middle of February, in consequence of the submission of the rulers of Lower Scinde. A bridge of boats had, in the meantime, been placed across the great river Indus, and the THIRTEENTH Light Infantry crossed this celebrated stream, to traverse regions which a British army had never before penetrated, but which are interesting from their association with ancient history, being the scene of the operations, and reverses of Alexander the Great, upwards of two thousand years since: after a march of four days they arrived at Shikarpore, when the difficulties of the enterprise began to assume a formidable character.

Advancing from Shikarpore the regiment proceeded through a desert country to Usted, and afterwards continued its route through the arid plains of Beloochistan, occasionally suffering inconvenience from the want of water, and from the predatory habits of the Beloochees, and arrived in the middle of March, at Dadur, situated a few miles from the Bolan Pass.

From Dadur the regiment continued its route; and

penetrating the Bolan Pass, marched between mountains covered with snow: in some places the pass was not more than seventeen yards wide, with gloomy crags rising perpendicularly in awful grandeur on each side. In these wild regions bands of Beloochees lurked to avail themselves of every opportunity to follow their predatory habits, and they murdered several camp followers, and plundered some baggage. Issuing from this gloomy defile of more than fifty miles in length, the regiment entered the Dusht-i be-doulut, or the unhappy-desert, and halted a short time at Quettah, situated in the centre of the valley of Shawl, of which it is the capital. Supplies of provisions could not be procured for the army in these sterile regions; the issue of grain for the horses ceased, the soldiers were placed upon half rations, the native followers upon quarter, and several men, who were searching for forage at a distance from the camp, were murdered by the ferocious natives, who hovered round the army to avail themselves of every opportunity of destroying small parties.

The soldiers bore all the hardships to which they were subjected with fortitude, and in the early part of April the army commenced its march through the vale of Shawl; it descended the picturesque height of Kotul full one thousand feet, into the valley of Koochlak; forded rivers; traversed a difficult country spangled with flowers of every hue, and passed the height of Kozak, where the soldiers had to drag the artillery over the precipice with ropes. The army, surmounting every obstacle with patient perseverance, continued to press forward; the rulers of western Affghanistan were struck with dismay at the appearance of the formidable British host, and they fled from the capital, leaving the country to the Sovereign whom the British were advancing to restore. As the army continued its march, various

1839 classes of individuals tendered their submission, and on the 27th of April the British troops arrived at Candahar, the capital of western Affghanistan, where the soldiers obtained provisions and repose. The tents were pitched in the grassy meadows, among enclosures covered with crops of grain. The watery exhalations from the low grounds proved injurious to the health of the men, and the great heat experienced in the tents, with a saline impregnation in the water, augmented the number of the sick.

Breaking up from Candahar on the 27th of June, to reduce the remainder of the Shah's dominions to obedience to his authority, the army advanced along a valley of dismal sterility to the Turnuk river; then proceeding up the right bank, traversed the country of the Western Ghilzees, and arrived in the vicinity of *Ghuznee*, a strong fortress garrisoned by three thousand Affghans under Prince Mahomed Hyder Khan, who were well provided with stores, and had determined on a desperate defence: they had blocked up every gate by masonry excepting one.

The army having arrived before Ghuznee without a battering train of sufficient power to proceed by the regular method of breaching the walls, &c., the commander of the forces, Lieut.-General Sir John Keane, resolved to storm the place without delay. On the 21st July, a company of the THIRTEENTH under Captain Sutherland accompanied Captain Thomson, Bengal Engineers (Chief Engineer) on his reconnoitre, and had one man killed, and two wounded. During the night of the 22nd of July a quantity of gunpowder was brought secretly to the gate which was not blocked up by masonry, and which was destroyed by an explosion before daylight on the following morning.

To the THIRTEENTH was assigned the duty of covering the operations, in blowing open the gate, and they paraded at two o'clock, A.M. The regiment proceeded in advance of the storming party to the causeway of the gate, under cover of the darkness of the night, and the fire of the batteries of the assailants. Six men of the leading company were told off to assist in carrying the powder bags. On reaching the causeway, the THIRTEENTH extended in light order, along the ditch, and by their fire distracted the enemy's attention from the gate. After the explosion a company of the regiment, under Lieutenant Jennings, moved up with the Engineer Officer to ascertain if the operation had been attended with success; on which the light company of Her Majesty's Second regiment of foot, No. 9 company of the THIRTEENTH under Captain Vigors,—the light companies of Her Majesty's seventeenth and of the Bengal European Regiment, which had been named to form the advance of the storming column, immediately pressed forward under the command of Brigadier Dennie of the THIRTEENTH, and under a heavy fire, gallantly gained an entrance into the fort. These were quickly followed by the main storming column under Brigadier Sale (who was severely wounded on this occasion), of which the THIRTEENTH formed part, having been ordered to close on the advance of the four companies; and the whole were soon established in possession of the fort.

The THIRTEENTH and seventeenth regiments were directed against the citadel, which was found evacuated by the enemy. Large supplies of grain, ammunition of all kinds, and several guns and military weapons, with about two thousand horses, fell into the hands of the victors. A company of the regiment under Lieutenant Arthur Wilkinson succeeded in capturing the

1839 redoubt (or outwork), and took two standards and about sixty prisoners.

The distinguished conduct of Brigadier Sale was highly commended by the Commander in Chief Lieut-General Sir John Keane; and Brigadier Dennie, Major Tronson, and Captain Kershaw were distinguished in the despatches. The regiment had one man killed, and three serjeants and twenty-seven rank and file wounded.

When the Affghan horsemen, who had assembled in the neighbourhood, learnt the fate of the fortress, they abandoned their camp equipage and baggage, and fled towards Cabool, the capital of eastern Affghanistan, in the direction of which city the British forces immediately advanced.

Dost Mahomed Khan, the ruler of the country, assembled a formidable host in position near Ughundee; but ascertaining that his soldiers had resolved to abandon him, he fled with a body of select cavalry, leaving his artillery in position; and the British army, advancing by triumphant marches to the capital, replaced Shah-Shoojah-ool-Moolk in the possession of the palace of his forefathers, from which he had been an exile many years. The conquest of a kingdom was thus achieved, by British skill and enterprise, with trifling loss, and the army pitched its tents in a rich valley near the capital.

The services of the THIRTEENTH Light Infantry were afterwards rewarded with the royal authority to bear on their regimental colour the words "AFFGHANISTAN" and "GHUZNEE." A medal was given by the restored monarch to the officers and soldiers present at the storming of Ghuznee, which Her Majesty QUEEN VICTORIA authorized them to receive and wear. An order of merit was also instituted by the Shah, called

REGIMENT OF LIGHT INFANTRY. 83

the ORDER of the " DOORANÉE EMPIRE," the decorations 1839 of which were conferred on the general and field officers; and Her Majesty was graciously pleased to grant permission to Sir Robert Sale, of the THIRTEENTH, to accept and wear the insignia of the first class, and Brevet Major James Kershaw and Captain Hamlet Wade the insignia of the third class of the order. Colonel Robert Henry Sale, was promoted to the rank of Major General in Affghanistan, and was appointed by Her Majesty to be a Knight Commander of the Most Honorable Military Order of the Bath; Major Edward T. Tronson was promoted to the rank of lieut.-colonel in the army, and Captain James Kershaw to that of major, for their services in this campaign ; the promotions taking place from the 23rd July, 1839, the date of the capture of Ghuznee.

NAMES of the officers of the THIRTEENTH who received the Ghuznee Medal :—

Brigadier Robert Henry Sale.
——— William Dennie.

Major Edward Tronson.
——-- Tristram Squire.

Captains.

George Fothergill.
William Sutherland.
James Kershaw.
Robert Pattisson.

John Taylor.
Horatio Vigors.
Henry Havelock.

Lieutenants.

Arthur Wilkinson.
James Fenwick.
John Foulston.
Peter Jennings.
Philip Von Streng.
Alexander Holcombe.
George King.

Rollo Burslem.
John Wood.
Frederick Holder.
William Sinclair
Hon. Emilius Forester.
Thomas Oxley.
David Rattray.

Ensigns.

Edward King.
George Mein.

Richard Frere.
George Wade.

Paymaster Harry Carew.—*Adjutant* Hamlet Wade.
Assistant Surgeons J. Robertson, M.D. and G. Barnes, M.D.

1839 A complete change had been achieved in the aspect of affairs beyond the Indus; the chiefs of Cabool and Candahar, who had entertained hostile designs against the British interest, had been deprived of power, and the territories they ruled had been restored to a friendly monarch. These splendid results accomplished, part of the army was withdrawn from the country; but the THIRTEENTH Light Infantry were selected to remain in Affghanistan, to support the government of the restored Shah, against the machinations of the chiefs who had usurped his authority during his exile.

The regiment was encamped near Cabool until November, when it marched into garrison at the Bala Hissar, or citadel of Cabool, in which stands the palace, with the thirty-fifth native infantry, and a detail of artillery, and remained there during the winter, which was an unusually severe season. Brigadier Dennie commanded the garrison, and Lieutenant Hamlet C. Wade, who had been selected by Lieut.-General Lord Keane to serve on the general staff of the army, was appointed major of brigade to this force.

1840 In May, the regiment moved into camp much reduced in numbers, having suffered very severely from disease. On the 24th September it was again called upon to take the field, having been attached to the force, under Sir Robert Sale, directed against Dost Mahomed in the Kohistan of Cabool; and it marched that day.

On the 29th September, the regiment under Lieut.-Colonel Tronson assisted in carrying the town and forts of *Tootumdurra*, at the entrance of the Ghorebund Pass, occupied by Ali Khan, a refractory chief of the Kohistan. The loss of the THIRTEENTH was limited to two privates wounded; one mortally.

On the 3rd October, the regiment was again engaged 1840 with the enemy at *Julgar*, about sixteen miles from Charekar, and although the attack of the storming party on the fort was not successful, yet Lieut.-Colonel Tronson, commanding the storming party, and Brevet Major Kershaw, Lieutenant and Adjutant Wood, Lieutenants Edward King, and George Wade (the four latter officers having at one time attained the crest of the breach) highly distinguished themselves, and were particularly mentioned by Major-General Sir Robert Sale in his despatch, who also acknowledged the assistance he received from his major of brigade, Captain Hamlet Wade. The scaling-ladders, hastily constructed from the poles used in carrying the litters for the sick, were of little use ; no sooner did the soldiers attempt to ascend them, than they sank into the soft débris on which they were planted : under these circumstances the storming party retired, leaving the Serjeant-Major of the Regiment (Airey) and fourteen men lying dead under the walls. Serjeant Hurst, of the THIRTEENTH, unable to move from his wounds, was carried off by Lieutenant King; and a Sepoy was, in like manner, conveyed to the rear by private Thomas Robinson of the regiment, under a most terrific fire. Lieutenant and Adjutant Wood, three serjeants, two corporals, and twelve privates were wounded.

It was subsequently determined to renew the attack, when it might be made by a combined movement against the breach, gateway, and wicket, with better chances of success, but the enemy, however, notwithstanding the precautions taken to intercept them, succeeded in escaping from the fort before seven o'clock P. M., at which hour the British took possession of it, and measures were taken for its destruction.

86 THE THIRTEENTH, OR PRINCE ALBERT'S

1840 The THIRTEENTH came again in contact with the enemy on the 19th October at *Babookooshghur*, when they were attacked in camp at night, but experienced little loss. On the 2nd November, the regiment was engaged with the Affghans at *Purwan*, where they had taken up a strong position under Dost Mahomed, who however retired from the field, and delivered himself up to the authorities at Cabool, when the purposes for which the force commenced operations being effected, it was directed to return to Cabool, and the THIRTEENTH took possession of the new cantonments there on the 8th November.

1841 After having been nearly three years on active service, the regiment was in expectation of commencing its march back to India, in October 1841; but at this period the government of Shah Shoojah became so unpopular, that the Affghans appeared determined to effect, by violence or circumvention, the expulsion of the British, by whose aid he had been reinstated in the sovereignty of Cabool.

A body of insurgents having possessed themselves of the *Khoord Cabool* pass, about ten miles from the capital, impeded the communication with India, when the first Lieut.-Colonel of the regiment, Major-General SIR ROBERT SALE, K.C.B., was detached with a small force, of which the THIRTEENTH Light Infantry formed part, to expel the rebels and re-open the communication. The regiment left Cabool on the 11th of October; the pass was forced on the following morning, and the troops penetrated to Khoord Cabool.* The regiment had

---

* Captain .H C. Wade accompanied the force as Head of the Staff, and Captain H. Havelock, who had been appointed Persian Interpreter to the Major-General commanding in Affghanistan, volunteered his services as aide-de-camp to Sir Robert Sale, who expressed his satisfaction of their conduct in his public despatch.

three men killed and twenty-four wounded on this occasion:—Major-General Sir Robert Sale, Captain H. C. Wade (Major of Brigade), Lieutenant George Mein, and Ensign Oakes were wounded. Lieutenant Mein being dangerously wounded, was obliged to be sent back in a litter to Cabool. Upon Sir Robert Sale being obliged to quit the field from the severity of his wound, the command of the troops devolved on Lieut.-Colonel Dennie, C.B. of the THIRTEENTH. The regiment then faced about, to return through the pass according to the plan for executing the operation, leaving the other corps at Khoord Cabool. Possession was then taken of Bootkhak, where the regiment was stationed from the 12th to the 18th of October. During this delay, the corps was much harassed by incessant night-attacks from the enemy, called by them Shub Khoon (Night Slaughter), which caused it some loss, but by Sir Robert Sale's precaution in ordering the men to lie down on their alarm posts, as soon as the enemy's fire was opened on the camp, much loss was prevented. The orders prohibiting any return-fire from the troops saved much, and all the attempts of the enemy to force an entrance into camp were successfully resisted by the bayonet alone. Meanwhile the rebellion continued of a formidable character, and the THIRTEENTH Light Infantry were ordered to march to *Tezeen*, where they arrived on the 22nd of October and were engaged with a body of insurgents, whom they drove from some heights and strong positions. The regiment on this duty had the misfortune to lose Lieutenant Edward King, who fell at the head of his company, while gallantly charging the enemy. Lieutenant R. E. Frere was wounded: the other casualties were three privates killed, and nine rank and file wounded.

1811   In consequence of orders from Cabool, the force under Major-General Sir Robert Sale marched for *Gundamuck*, and were continually pressed day and night, by insurgent bands hovering on their flanks and rear, which occasioned the fatigues and duties of the troops to be particularly harassing; the way led along defiles and over mountains, and when the soldiers halted, breastworks had to be thrown up to defend the bivouac ground from sudden attacks of the Affghan cavalry.

On the 29th of October the rebels were found in force at the *Jugdulluck* Pass, and for some time they checked the advance of the column; but the skirmishers of the THIRTEENTH Light Infantry, sprang forward with distinguished gallantry, and driving the Affghans from almost inaccessible heights protected by breast-works, enabled the British force to surmount every obstacle in he defile, and to arrive at Gundamuck on the following day. Lieutenants P. R. Jennings, A. E. F. Holcombe, and David Rattray were severely wounded on this service; four privates were killed, and forty-two wounded. Lieut.-Colonel Dennie, Captains Wilkinson, Havelock, Wade, (Brigade-Major) and Fenwick, were specially mentioned by Major-General Sir Robert Sale in his despatch.

The troops under Major-General Sir Robert Sale remained at Gundamuck until the 5th November, when they proceeded and captured the fort of *Mamoo Khail* in the neighbourhood, and returned on the 6th to Gundamuck; there intelligence was received of the breaking out of a violent insurrection at Cabool, on the 2nd of November, and of the probability that the rebellion would become general. Under these circumstances, two forced marches on Jellalabad were made, with a numerous enemy pressing on the flanks and rear; a body of insurgents were beaten at *Futtehabad* by the rear-guard under Lieut-Colonel Dennie; and *Jellalabad,* 1841 the chief town in the valley of Ningrahar, was seized by the British troops on the 12th November, to establish a post upon which the corps at Cabool might retire, if necessary, and to restore a link in the chain of communication with India. The Affghan irregulars, left at Gundamuck, revolted, and a general rising took place among the tribes.

Major-General Sir Robert Sale, on taking possession of Jellalabad, found the fortress in a very dilapidated state, and the inhabitants disaffected to the government of the Shah. The Affghans collected to about ten thousand, and the walls of the fort being without parapets, and the garrison having only one day and a half supplies, on half rations, a sally was made on the 14th November, which routed the enemy, and enabled the troops to collect provisions, and erect works for the defence of the fortress. On this latter duty, the THIRTEENTH Light Infantry were conspicuous for the alacrity and indefatigable perseverance they evinced under circumstances of the most disheartening and trying character. The demolition of ruinous forts and old walls, filling up ravines, destroying gardens, cutting down groves, raising the parapets to six or seven feet high, repairing and widening the ramparts, extending the bastions, retrenching three of the gates, covering the fourth with an outwork, and excavating a ditch ten feet in depth and twelve in width round the whole of the walls, were works of great labour, which called forth the efforts of every individual. While thus employed another array of many thousands of Affghans on the 27th of November again invested the place, but they were completely routed and dispersed by a sally of the garrison on the 1st December.

1842 On the 9th of January, 1842, the garrison was summoned to give up the fortress, by the leader of the Affghan rebellion, in fulfilment of a convention entered into at Cabool; but Major-General Sir Robert Sale, being fully assured of the bad faith of the insurgents, refused; the annihilation of the troops from the capital, in the Ghilzie defiles, by the severity of the climate, and the basest treachery on the part of those in whose promises they had confided, proved the correctness of the major-general's estimation of the Affghan character.

By the indefatigable exertions of the troops, under the direction of Captain Broadfoot, garrison engineer, and Captain Abbott, commissary of ordnance, the works were brought into a state of defence against any Asiatic enemy not provided with siege-artillery; but the place was kept in a continual state of alarm by the occurrence of one hundred shocks of an earthquake in the course of a month, and on the 19th of February a tremendous shock occasioned the parapets to fall, injured the bastions, made a breach in the rampart, destroyed the guard-houses, reduced other portions of the works to ruins, and demolished one-third part of the town. With that unconquerable spirit of perseverance for which the troops had already been distinguished, they instantly turned to the repair of the works. Sirdar Mahomed Akbar Khan, Barukzye, the assassin of the late Envoy, and the treacherous destroyer of the Cabool force, flushed with success, approached with a numerous body of troops to overwhelm the little garrison of Jellalabad: he attacked the foraging parties on the 21st and 22nd of February; but was astonished at finding the works in a state of defence, and he established a rigorous blockade. From that time to the 7th of April, the reduced garrison was engaged in a succession of skirmishes, in which 1842 the THIRTEENTH Light Infantry had opportunities of distinguishing themselves; particularly detachments under Captains Pattisson and Fenwick, Lieutenants George Wade and W. Cox.

On the 5th April, 1842, information was received that the force under Major-General Pollock had experienced reverses in the Khyber, and had retraced its steps towards Peshawur; and on the 6th a *feu-de-joie* and salute of artillery were fired by Mahomed Akbar, which were stated to be in honour of the event. It was also reported that the Affghans were sending reinforcements to assist in defending their frontier passes. These reports were accompanied by others of a fresh revolution at Cabool, which was considered by some as the cause of the rejoicing; and it was also rumoured that the Ghazees had been defeated in Khyber, and that the Sirdar had retreated into Lughman. Major-General Sir Robert Sale resolved to anticipate the last-mentioned event, by a general attack on the Affghan camp, with the hope of relieving Jellalabad from blockade, and facilitating General Pollock's advance to its succour. Directions were accordingly given to form three columns of infantry, the central consisting of the THIRTEENTH (mustering five hundred bayonets) under Colonel Dennie, C. B.; the left consisting of a similar number of the thirty-fifth native infantry under Lieut.-Colonel Monteath, C.B.; and the right composed of one company of the THIRTEENTH, one of the thirty-fifth native infantry, and the detachment of Sappers under the command of Lieutenant Orr (the severity of Captain Broadfoot's wound still rendering him non-effective), amounting to three hundred and sixty men, was commanded by Captain

Havelock of the THIRTEENTH; these were to be supported by the fire of the guns of number 6 field battery under Captain Abbott, the whole of the small cavalry force being under Captain Oldfield and Lieutenant Mayne.

At daylight, on the morning of the 7th April, the troops issued from the Cabool and Peshawur gates. The Sirdar, Mahomed Akbar Khan, with his force of about six thousand men, was formed in order of battle for the defence of his camp; its right resting on a fort, and its left on the Cabool river; even the ruined works within eight hundred yards of the place, recently repaired, were filled with Ghilzie marksmen, who were evidently prepared for a stout resistance. The attack was led by the skirmishers and column under Captain Havelock, which drove the enemy in the most satisfactory manner from the extreme left of his advanced line of works, which it pierced at once, and proceeded to advance into the plain; the central column at the same time directed its efforts against a square fort, upon the same base, the defence of which was obstinately maintained. Colonel Dennie of the THIRTEENTH, while nobly leading his regiment to the assault, received a shot through his body, which, to the deep regret of officers and men, shortly after proved fatal.

The rear of the work having been finally gained by passing to its left, orders were given for a combined attack upon the enemy's camp; this was brilliant and successful. The artillery advanced at the gallop, and directed a heavy fire upon the Affghan centre, while two columns of infantry penetrated his line near the same point, and the third forced back his left from its support on the river, into which some of his horse and foot were driven. The Affghans repeatedly attempted to check the advance by a smart fire of musketry,—by throwing forward heavy bodies of horse, which twice threatened in force the detachments of infantry under Captain Havelock, and by opening three guns, screened by a garden wall, which were said to have been served under the personal superintendence of the Sirdar; but in a short time the Affghans were dislodged from every point of their positions, their cannon taken, and their camp involved in a general conflagration.

1842

The battle was over, and the enemy in full retreat in the direction of Lughman by about seven, A.M. Two cavalry standards were taken from the enemy, besides four guns lost by the Cabool army and Gundamuck forces, the recapture of which was a matter of much honest exultation. A great quantity of *matériel* and stores were, together with the enemy's tents, destroyed, and the defeat of Mahomed Akbar, in open field, by the troops he had boasted of blockading, was complete.

The regiment had Colonel Dennie killed, and Lieutenant Jennings and Assistant-Surgeon Barnes wounded; eight privates killed, and thirty-one rank and file wounded.

Captain Wilkinson, of the THIRTEENTH, on whom the charge of one of the infantry columns devolved on the lamented fall of Colonel Dennie, and Captain Hamlet Wade (Brigade Major), were highly commended in Major-General Sir Robert Sale's despatch, in which it was also stated ' that Lieutenant and Adjutant Wood, ' Her Majesty's THIRTEENTH Light Infantry, made a ' dash at one of the enemy, and in cutting him down, ' his charger was so severely injured as to have been ' since destroyed. Captain Havelock reports in the

1842 'most favourable manner the gallant conduct, through-
'out the day, of Lieutenant Cox, Her Majesty's THIR-
'TEENTH Light Infantry, and he was the first of the
'party which captured them to seize two of the enemy's
'cannon.'

Armourer Serjeant Henry Ulyett, of the THIR-
TEENTH, captured Mahomed Akbar's standard, which
he took from a cavalry soldier, whom he killed.

The force employed in this successful enterprise
amounted to about eighteen hundred men of all arms.
The safety of the fortress was entrusted, during the
action, to the ordinary guards of its gates, and one
provisional battalion of followers of every description
armed with pikes and other weapons, who manned the
curtains, and made a respectable show of defence.
Captain Pattisson, of the THIRTEENTH, was left in command of this diminished garrison. Towards the conclusion of the engagement a sally was made from the
Cabool gate by Lieutenant George Wade, of the THIR-
TEENTH, into the fort before which Colonel Dennie had
fallen, when it was observed that the enemy were aban-
doning it; all it contained was set on fire, and some of
its defenders were bayoneted.

The enemy's loss was very severe; the field of battle
was strewed with the bodies of men and horses, and
the richness of the trappings of some of the latter de-
noted that chiefs of rank (several being present and
taking part in the action) had fallen.

The following NOTIFICATION of this victory was
issued by the Government of India from Benares on
the 21st April, 1842:—

'The Governor General feels assured that every
'subject of the British Government will peruse with
'the deepest interest and satisfaction the report he

'now communicates, of the entire defeat of the Affghan 1842
'troops under Mahomed Akbar Khan, by the garrison
'of Jellalabad.

'That *Illustrious Garrison*, which, by its constancy in
'enduring privation, and by its valour in action, has
'already obtained for itself the sympathy and respect
'of every true soldier, has now, sallying forth from its
'walls, under the command of its gallant leader, Major-
'General Sir Robert Sale, thoroughly beaten in open
'field an enemy of more than three times its numbers,
'taken the standards of their boasted cavalry, destroyed
'their camp, and recaptured four guns, which, under
'circumstances which can never again occur, had during
'the last winter fallen into their hands.

'The Governor General cordially congratulates the
'army upon the return of victory to its ranks.

'He is convinced that there, as in all former times,
'it will be found, while, as at Jellalabad, the European
'and native troops mutually supporting each other,
'and evincing equal discipline and valour, are led into
'action by officers in whom they justly confide.

'The Governor General directs that the substance
'of this notification, and of Major-General Sir Robert
'Sale's report, be carefully made known to all the
'troops, and that a salute of twenty-one guns be fired
'at every principal station of the army.'

On the 20th February following, the thanks of
Parliament were accorded to the Governor General of
India, and to the officers and troops employed in
Affghanistan, the resolutions being moved in the House
of Lords by the Duke of Wellington, and in the House
of Commons by Sir Robert Peel, who, after eulogising
the gallant conduct of Sir Robert Sale and the garrison
of Jellalabad, proceeded to deplore the death of Colonel

Dennie, in the victory of the 7th April, in the following terms:—

'That victory would have been the cause of almost 'unqualified rejoicing if it had not been purchased at 'the cost of the life of one of the most noble and gallant 'spirits, whose actions have ever added brilliance to 'their country's military renown. Need I mention 'the name of the lamented Colonel Dennie? With 'his accustomed valour,—a valour which was un- 'quenchable,—he led the British troops against the 'enemy. The attack which he headed was successful, 'but he fell in the conflict; and a spirit as gallant as 'his own has offered to his family and his friends that 'which he thinks,—and justly thinks,—the highest con- 'solation that can be afforded them. "True it is," he 'says, "he has lost his life; but he lost his life on the 'field of battle, and in the hour of victory!" Such is 'the consolation which Sir Robert Sale offers to his 'bereaved family and friends. I wish it had been 'possible—but it was not—I wish it had been possible 'that the dying moments of Colonel Dennie could have 'been consoled, as I believe they would have been, by 'the knowledge that, on account of the former valour 'and intrepidity he had displayed,—he having no other 'interest or influence than that just interest and in- 'fluence which such courage and devotion ought always 'to command,—the Queen of England had signified her 'personal wish that Colonel Dennie should be appointed 'one of her aides-de-camp. I sincerely wish that 'Colonel Dennie could have been made acquainted 'with this fact.' *

The defence of Jellalabad, situated amid scenery of

* It is gratifying to be able to state, that Colonel Dennie's appointment as aide-de-camp to the Queen was known at the regiment about a week previous to his lamented fall.

wild and savage grandeur, against an undisciplined but desperate enemy, who used his rude implements of war with deadly precision, will ever excite the highest admiration, and the British nation owes a lasting debt of gratitude to Major-General Sir Robert Sale, and the gallant band of heroes composing the garrison. These successes, contrasting so forcibly with the unforeseen disasters at Cabool, which partook more of the character of a hideous dream than of stern reality, may well make the THIRTEENTH refer with honest pride to the part they bore in these achievements.

On the 16th June, 1842, the Queen was graciously pleased to appoint Colonel Sir Robert Henry Sale (serving with the rank of Major-General in Affghanistan) to be a Knight Grand Cross of the Most Honorable Military Order of the Bath.

Major Edward T. Tronson was promoted to the rank of Lieut.-Colonel, in succession to Lieut.-Colonel Dennie, and Captain Robert Pattisson was advanced to the Majority. Lieut.-Colonel Tronson retired on full pay on the 2nd August, 1842, and was succeeded by Major Squire, and Captain John Taylor was promoted to the vacant rank of Major.

In a few days after this victory, the privations and sufferings of the garrison, from incessant toil and the deficiency of provisions, were terminated by the arrival of the force under Major-General Pollock, who, in his despatch of the 19th April, 1842, stated that, ' I have
' had an opportunity of inspecting the works thrown
' up for their protection by the indefatigable exertions
' of Sir Robert Sale's force, and my surprise at their
' strength and extent has been only equalled by my
' admiration of the excellent arrangements which must
' have pervaded all departments, since, after a siege

1842 '(by greatly superior numbers) of upwards of five months' duration, I find the garrison in excellent health and spirits, and in an admirable state of discipline, with a good supply of ammunition, ready and anxious to take the field, and most willing to advance on Cabool.'

Major-General Sir Robert Sale's report of the transactions in which the garrison of Jellalabad had been engaged, gives the following interesting particulars:—

'From the time that the brigade threw itself into Jellalabad, the native troops have been on half, and the followers on quarter rations, and for many weeks they have been able to obtain little or nothing in the bazaars to eke out this scanty provision. I will not mention, as a privation, the European troops from the same period having been without their allowance of spirits, because I verily believe this circumstance and their constant employment have contributed to keep them in the highest health and the most remarkable state of discipline. Crime has been almost unknown amongst them, but they have felt severely, although they have never murmured, the diminution of their quantity of animal food, and the total want of ghee, flour, tea, coffee, and sugar: these may seem small matters to those who read of them at a distance, but they are serious reductions in the scale of comfort of the hard-working and fighting soldier in Asia. The troops have also been greatly in arrears of pay, besides their severe duties in heat and cold, wind and rain, on the guards of the gates and bastions. The troops, officers and men, British and Hindoostanee, of every arm, remained fully accoutred on their alarm posts every night from the 1st of March to the 7th April.

'The losses of officers and men, in carriage and cattle,
'camp equipage and baggage, between Cabool and
'Jellalabad were heavy; and their expenditure, during
'the siege and blockade, in obtaining articles of mere
'subsistence and necessity, has been exorbitant.

'It is gratifying to me to forward the opinion of my
'second in command, Lieut.-Colonel Monteath, C.B.,
'placed on record without solicitation, of the merits of
'the THIRTEENTH LIGHT INFANTRY, of which corps I
'am proud of being a member. * * * I must express my
'gratitude to Providence for having placed so gallant
'and devoted a force under my command; in every
'way it has exceeded my most sanguine expectations,
'and I beg leave, in the strongest manner, to solicit the
'interposition of Major-General Pollock, C.B., who has
'nobly labored and fought to relieve it from its critical
'position in the midst of a hostile empire, in now com-
'mitting it to the protection and favour of the Right
'Honorable the Governor General in Council, and
'through him to the Court of Directors, and of our
'Sovereign.'

Lieut.-Colonel Monteath stated in his report,—As
'doing but due justice on this occasion to Her Majesty's
'THIRTEENTH Light Infantry might be looked upon
'as a highly-coloured record of the merits of your own
'regiment, and seeing that no such partial bias can
'possibly be supposed to guide my feelings in the es-
'timate I have formed of their deserts, I have pleasure
'in sincerely declaring, that *their conduct, throughout the*
'*painful and perilous position in which we have so long been*
'*placed, has been such as fully to deserve the applause and*
'*admiration of their country, and the confidence and best*
'*consideration of our well-beloved Sovereign.*

'On our throwing ourselves, on the 12th November

'last, into the old and ruined town of Jellalabad, without money, without food, and almost without protection, with a nation of highly excited and barbarous enemies in arms against us, our situation seemed as hopeless a one as British troops were ever called upon to confront; notwithstanding which, the enemy was twice attacked within twenty days, and on both occasions defeated with signal success.

'You, yourself, will doubtless detail the works performed by the regiment; let it then be only my province, who have witnessed their exertions, almost hourly during a period of five months, to record, that *their devoted perseverance and cheerfulness amidst all the gloom that surrounded them, after the destruction of their comrades of the Cabool force, could not have been surpassed by any troops in the world;* and that after months of extreme toil, when an earthquake, such as man is not often in the habit of experiencing, in a moment left scarcely a vestige of their labour standing; *their flying as they did with redoubled zeal to the work, and completing it in ten days,* (so that on the arrival of the enemy before Jellalabad, they declared that the calamity which had befallen the valley arose from nothing but English witchcraft, it being the only place that had escaped uninjured) *was what none but British soldiers could have performed, and what no price could have purchased,* for it was the labour of the heart, work of all others most deserving of distinction and reward.'

The distinguished conduct of the regiment was appreciated, and Her Majesty thus alluded to it in her most gracious speech on proroguing Parliament on the 12th August, 1842 :—' Although I have had deeply to lament the reverses which have befallen a division of the army to the westward of the Indus, yet I have the

'satisfaction of reflecting that the gallant defence of
' the city of Jellalabad, crowned by a decisive victory
' in the field, has eminently proved the courage and
' discipline of the European and Native troops, and
' the skill and fortitude of their distinguished com-
' mander.'

On the 26th of August, the pleasure of Her Majesty the Queen Victoria, was officially announced in the London Gazette:—

' *War Office*, 26*th August*, 1842.

' In consideration of the distinguished gallantry dis-
' played by the THIRTEENTH Light Infantry during
' the campaigns in the Burmese empire and in Affghan-
' istan, Her Majesty has been graciously pleased to
' approve of that regiment assuming the title of the
' THIRTEENTH OR PRINCE ALBERT'S REGIMENT OF
' LIGHT INFANTRY; and of its facings being changed
' from *yellow* to *blue*.

' Her Majesty has also been pleased to authorize the
' THIRTEENTH Regiment of Light Infantry to bear on
' its colours and appointments a ' *Mural Crown*,' super-
' scribed ' *Jellalabad*,' as a memorial of the fortitude,
' perseverance, and enterprise, evinced by that regi-
' ment, and the several corps which served during the
' blockade of Jellalabad.

' Her Majesty has been likewise pleased to permit
' the THIRTEENTH regiment to receive and wear a *silver*
' *medal*, which has been directed by the Governor
' General of India to be distributed to every officer,
' non-commissioned officer, and private, European and
' Native,—who belonged to the garrison of Jellalabad
' on the 7th April, 1842;—such medals to bear on one
' side a ' *Mural Crown*,' superscribed ' *Jellalabad ;*' and
' on the other side ' *April 7th*, 1842.' '

1842   The medal for Jellalabad was granted to the following officers of the THIRTEENTH:—

Lieutenant-Colonels.
Colonel Sir Robert Sale, G.C.B.
—— William H. Dennie, C.B.*

Major.
Robert Pattisson.

Captains.

Henry Havelock.
Arthur P. S. Wilkinson.
Hamlet C. Wade.

James H. Fenwick.
Peter R. Jennings.

Lieutenants.

Alex. E. F. Holcombe.
George King.
John S. Wood, (*Adjutant.*)
Wm. A. Sinclair.
Hon. E. J. W. Forester.
David Rattray.
Richard E. Frere.
George Wade.

John Wm. Cox.
William Williams.
Fred. Van Straubenzee.
Thos. B. Speedy.
J. Francis Scott.
G. Chetwynd Stapylton.
Robt. S. Parker

Ensigns.

Arthur Oakes. | Geo. Talbot.

Surgeon, Jno. Robertson, *M.D.*   *Assist.-Surg.* G. W. Barnes, *M.D.*

The regiment remained in garrison at Jellalabad until the 6th August, when it moved forwards to Futtehabad for change of air, having suffered severely from the extreme heat of the weather. So great was the heat, that six men fell dead in the ranks of apoplexy the first march. On the 1st of September, the THIRTEENTH received orders to join the force under

* The following interesting circumstance was related by Lord Fitzgerald and Vesey in the House of Lords, in his speech on the 20th February, 1843, regarding the vote of thanks for the operations in Affghanistan. The Adjutant General of the Army in India, acting by the command of Lord Ellenborough, transmitted to the aged mother of Colonel Dennie that medal which her son would have worn, had he happily survived. In replying to the letter which accompanied this token Mrs. Dennie beautifully said, that she accepted it with pleasure and with pride, for she had a right to feel a ' pride in her son's life, and in his death.' Lord Fitzgerald added, that it was impossible to read that passage without honoring the lady, and even more deeply lamenting the fate of the son of whom she had so justly and truly written.

Major-General Pollock at Gundamuck, to which place 1842 the regiment marched on the following morning, and joined on the 3rd. It remained there until the 7th, when it moved towards Cabool, forming part of the first division of the advance, which was placed under the command of Major General Sir Robert Sale. On the 8th, upon nearing *Jugdulluck*, the Affghans were observed in position, and the THIRTEENTH under Captain Wilkinson were directed to carry the left centre of the enemy, which was done in gallant style. The enemy were dispersed in every direction, a large body of them retiring to the summit of a high mountain. On this rugged and almost inaccessible height they planted their standards, but as the achievements of the day would have been incomplete were they suffered to remain, it was decided to dislodge them. The lofty heights were assaulted in two columns, the THIRTEENTH being led by Captain Wilkinson, and the Ghilzies fled from their last and least assailable stronghold. Major General Sir Robert Sale was again wounded. The other casualties of the regiment were one private killed and two serjeants and twelve privates wounded.

The THIRTEENTH bivouacked in the valley of Jugdulluck, which was strewn with the blackened remains of their unfortunate comrades of the Cabool force. Near this place Brevet Major Kershaw and Lieutenant Hobhouse of the THIRTEENTH were killed in January 1842, while retiring with the force from Cabool. The enemy showed no opposition to the advance of the army until nearing the valley of *Tezeen*, when some skirmishing took place, and the troops halted in the valley a day to allow the rear division of the advance to close up. The road from Tezeen to Khoord Cabool was through a succession of lofty hills, called the Huft

Kotul, or Eight Hills. Dispositions for the attack of the *Huft Kotul Pass* having been made on the 12th of September, the force moved off on the following morning, and three companies of the THIRTEENTH formed part of the advance guard under Sir Robert Sale. To them was allotted the duty of clearing the right of the Pass, which was effectively done. A company under Lieutenant W. A. Sinclair, which formed part of the force placed under Major Skinner of the thirty-first regiment, and which was detached on the right of the pass, also distinguished itself.

The regiment lost one rank and file killed, and had five wounded. The enemy's loss was heavy; he was completely defeated, and left his artillery in the possession of the victors. The army re-occupied Cabool on the 15th September, and on the 18th, part of the regiment received sudden orders to march with the force under Major-General Sir Robert Sale in order to meet the prisoners lately in possession of the enemy, then on their way to Cabool, it being supposed that Akbar Khan would attempt to re-capture them. On the morning of the 20th, the troops met the prisoners (Lady Sale and Lieutenant Mein* being among them), and on the 21st returned with them to Cabool, without being annoyed by the enemy. The regiment remained

---

* Sir Robert Peel, on moving the vote of thanks to the army employed in Affghanistan, on the 20th February, 1843, alluded in the following terms to Lieutenant Mein's conduct, while serving with the army on its retreat from Cabool:—" I have said that, in the course of this campaign, instances of the most generous devotion, of friendly sympathy, and of desperate fidelity, were displayed, which deserve at least a passing notice. Lieutenant Eyre says : ' Lieutenant Sturt (son-in-law to Sir Robert and ' Lady Sale) had nearly cleared the defile, when he received his wound, ' and would have been left on the ground to be hacked to pieces by the ' Ghazees, who followed in the rear to complete the work of slaughter, but ' for the generous intrepidity of Lieutenant Mein of Her Majesty's THIR-' TEENTH Light Infantry, who, on learning what had befallen him, went ' back to his succour, and stood by him for several minutes, at the imminent

at Cabool until the 12th of October,* when the army 1842 broke ground on its return to India. The regiment shared in the many skirmishes on quitting the Affghan territory, but sustained little loss, and on the 24th, it reached Jellalabad; previously to proceeding further, it was considered advisable to destroy the fortress, and in a few days not a wall was left standing. On the south face of the fort was a large bastion, close to which was an open space which had been converted into a burial-ground; here the remains of Colonel Dennie, with many other gallant soldiers, were laid, and the Engineer Officer in mining the bastion, caused the whole mass to be thrown by the explosion over the graves, thus leaving a lasting monument over them, and what was of more importance, effectually preventing the bodies being disturbed by the Affghans. The regiment thence proceeded to Peshawur, and across the Punjaub *en route* to Ferozepore.

According to the wish of the Governor-General (Lord Ellenborough), the garrison of Jellalabad had received orders to proceed in advance of the rest of the troops, in order that they should make a triumphant entry

'risk of his own life, vainly entreating aid from the passers by. He was 'at length, joined by Serjeant Deane, of the Sappers, with whose assistance 'he dragged his friend, on a quilt, through the remainder of the Pass, when 'he succeeded in mounting him on a miserable pony, and conducted him 'in safety to the camp, where the unfortunate officer lingered till the fol- 'lowing morning, and was the only man of the whole force who received 'Christian burial. Lieutenant Mein was himself at this very time suffering 'from a dangerous wound in the head received in the previous October, 'and his heroic disregard of self, and fidelity to his friend in the hour of 'danger, are well deserving of a record in the annals of British valour and 'virtue; I think, Sir, it is but just that the name of Lieutenant Mein should 'be mentioned with honour in the House of Commons, and I do not regret 'having noticed this circumstance, as it has called forth so generous and 'general an expression of sympathy and approval.' "

* The regiment lost by death a very promising young officer, Lieutenant Scott, this night; and Lieutenant Frere also fell a victim to the fatigues and vicissitudes of the campaign on the 18th November, 1842.

1842 into the British Provinces by themselves, and the medals granted for the defence of, and general action near, Jellalabad, had been forwarded a few days previously, so that they might be worn on the entry of the garrison into Ferozepore. On the 14th December, the THIRTEENTH arrived at the right bank of the Sutlej, where they halted until the 17th, when they crossed the river by a bridge of boats. At the opposite side was erected, for the garrison to pass under, a triumphal arch, where they were met by Lord Ellenborough; the distance from the river to the camp was about six miles, and for the first three miles a sort of street was formed for the garrison to pass through, by placing elephants decked in their gayest trappings at intervals of about twenty paces; the remainder of the road was lined by the army of reserve encamped at Ferozepore, who presented arms as the garrison passed, the bands playing the "National Anthem:" in the evening the officers of the garrison were entertained at a magnificent banquet given by the Governor General.

These honours were rendered, agreeably to the concluding paragraph of the General Order by the Right Honorable the Governor General of India, dated Allahabad, 30th of April, 1842, which stated that—

'The Governor General will request His Excellency
' the Commander-in-Chief of the army to give instruc-
' tions, in due time, that the several corps composing
' the garrison of Jellalabad may, on their return to
' India, be received at all the stations on their route
' to their cantonments, by all the troops at such sta-
' tions, in review order, with presented arms.'

The regiment received the Queen's permission to bear on its colours and appointments the word " CABOOL, 1842," to commemorate its important services. Major Pattisson was promoted to the brevet rank of Lieut.-Colonel; Captains Havelock, Wilkinson, Wade, and Fenwick were promoted to the brevet rank of Major, and, with the following officers, received the silver medal for Cabool :—

Colonel Sir Robert Sale, G.C.B.

Captains.

Major Henry Havelock.	Captain Peter Jennings.
———- Arthur Wilkinson.	————— Alex. Holcombe.
——- Hamlet Wade.	————— George King.
——— James Fenwick.	

Majors Havelock, Wilkinson, and Wade were subsequently appointed by Her Majesty Companions of the most Honorable Military Order of the Bath.

Lieutenants.

John S. Wood (*adjutant*).	Fred. Van Straubenzee.
William A. Sinclair.	Thomas B. Speedy.
Hon. Emilius J. Forrester.	J. Fran. P. Scott.
David Rattray.	Granville Geo. C. Stapylton.
Richard E. Frere.	Robert S. Parker.
Geo. Wade.	Arthur Oakes.
John W. Cox.	George Talbot.

Surgeon, J. Robertson, M.D.—*Asst.-Surgeon*, Geo. Barnes, M.D.

On the 16th January, 1843, the regiment marched 1843 from Ferozepore, and arrived at Mowbarukpore on the 5th of February, where it remained encamped until the 9th of March, when it proceeded on its route to Kussowlie, at which station it remained until the 21st October. Fatigue parties were here daily employed for two hours in the cool of the morning or evening cutting and repairing roads, etc. On the 21st October, the regiment marched to Ferozepore *en route* to Scinde. On the 6th November, the regiment reached Loodianah, where percussion muskets were issued to it for the first time, and the old flint arms were given into store. It arrived at Ferozepore on the 15th

1843 November, embarked in boats for Sukkur, on the 24th, and reached its destination on the 20th December.

General Edward Morrison died on the 3rd December, 1843, and the vacant colonelcy of the THIRTEENTH was conferred on the 15th of that month on Sir Robert Sale; Major Horatio Nelson Vigors was promoted to the rank of Lieutenant-Colonel; and Captain R. M. Meredith succeeded to the Majority.

1844 On the 13th January, 1844, Lieut.-Colonel Squire joined with a draft of officers and men from England, and assumed the command of the regiment.

The THIRTEENTH moved from Sukkur, by wings, *en route* to Kurrachee during September, 1844; the left wing on the 4th and the head-quarter division on the 24th. The former arrived at Kurrachee on the 21st of September, and the latter on the 8th of October. The regiment suffered severely from sickness during the movement, owing to the malaria of Sukkur, having continually from two to three hundred in hospital daily. Preparatory to the regiment leaving Scinde, four hundred and forty-six of the men volunteered to corps serving in India. It embarked at Kurrachee for Bombay on board the Honorable East India Company's steamers Pluto and Sesostris on the 4th of December, arrived in the harbour of Bombay on the night of the 7th, and disembarked in the afternoon of the 8th of that month, being received by the Governor and military authorities of Bombay; the guard of honor presenting arms as the regiment passed, and the band striking up "See the conquering hero comes."—While the regiment was stationed at Bombay, it had the misfortune to lose Captain Sinclair, who had served throughout the campaign : he died of cholera after an

illness of a few hours: the soldiers however continued 1844
generally healthy.

The head-quarter division of the THIRTEENTH em- 1845
barked in the freight ship Cornwall, at Colaba, Bombay, under the command of Lieut.-Colonel Tristram
C. Squire, on the 20th March, 1845, and the second
division in the freight ship Boyne, on the same day,
under the command of Lieut.-Colonel Horatio Vigors.
The right wing disembarked at Gravesend on the 28th
July, and the second division arrived there on the 8th
August following, from whence it proceeded to Walmer
Barracks, in order to join the head-quarters, which
had marched thither from Chatham.

On the 10th March, 1846, Lieut.-General Sir Wil- 1846
liam Maynard Gomm, K.C.B., Governor and Commander-in-Chief of the Mauritius, was appointed
colonel of the THIRTEENTH, in succession to Sir Robert
Sale, who was killed at the battle of Moodkee, on the
18th December, 1845.

The regiment proceeded from Walmer to Portsmouth on the 27th April, 1846. Previous to the march
of the THIRTEENTH, a high testimonial of their
conduct, while stationed at Walmer, was received from
the Mayor and Magistrates of Deal. On Thursday, the
13th August, the THIRTEENTH had the gratification of
being presented with new colours by His Royal Highness the Prince Albert. The "*United Service Gazette*"
of Saturday, the 15th August, gave the following account of this interesting ceremony, which took place
on Southsea Common:—' His Royal Highness Prince
' Albert, wearing a Field Marshal's uniform, came over
' from Osborne-house in the royal yacht, accompanied
' by Colonel Wylde and a small retinue, all in uniform,
' and landed at the King's-stairs, in the Dockyard, at

1846 ' about a quarter to four o'clock. The Commander-
' in-Chief, Admiral Sir Charles Ogle, Bart., the Lieut.-
' Governor, Major-General the Hon. Sir Hercules
' Pakenham, K.C.B., and a brilliant staff of officers
' of both services, received his Royal Highness on
' landing, who immediately entered General Paken-
' ham's carriage, and was driven to the field, escorted
' by General Pakenham and staff on horseback, re-
' ceiving the shouts of welcome from the immense con-
' course of spectators who lined the road as he passed.
' Soon after three o'clock, the regiment took up its
' position on Southsea Common, in line, at open order,
' with the old colours in the centre. On the arrival of
' the Prince he was received with the customary
' honors. The regiment then formed three sides of a
' hollow square, the company told off as a guard for
' the new colours remaining in the centre of the open
' face. The Prince having alighted from the carriage,
' mounted his charger (which, together with five other
' beautiful animals, came down from the Royal mews
' to the George Hotel last night), rode along the line,
' inside and out, inspecting the troops, as they covered
' the ground, after which the Prince dismounted and
' entered the hollow square, accompanied by General
' Pakenham, Sir Charles Ogle, and staff, and stood un-
' covered while the Rev. G. R. Gleig, Chaplain
' General to the Forces, consecrated the colours, which,
' after this ceremony, were handed to the Prince by
' Lieut.-Colonel C. T. Van Straubenzee and Major
' Meredith. The Prince then handed them to the two
' senior ensigns (J. D. Longden and Melville Browne),
' who received them kneeling, and continued in that
' position whilst His Royal Highness addressed them
' in a brief but most spirited and soldierly manner, en-

'joining them to preserve their colours, never to allow
'them to be captured, but to emulate the conduct
'exhibited by the departed hero, Sir Robert Sale,
'whose absence was the only alloy to the gratification
'he felt in performing the august ceremony of the day.
'His Highness, in the course of his address, passed
'some high and well-deserved encomiums on Colonel
'Squire and the Thirteenth regiment, to which that
'gallant veteran replied—" I beg most respectfully to
'" return my most sincere though humble thanks for
'" the distinguished honor your Royal Highness has
'" just conferred upon this corps in the presentation
'" of new colours, and for the highly flattering manner
'" in which your Royal Highness has been pleased to
'" mention my name, in connection with its services
'" in India, and also for the gratifying encomiums
'" which you have passed on our late honored and
'" respected Commanders, Sir Robert Sale and
'" Colonel Dennie. Your Highness may be assured
'" that your gracious condescension will ever be es-
'" teemed by all ranks in the regiment as the greatest
'" stimulant to the loyal and faithful discharge of
'" their duty, under whatever circumstances of trial
'" they may hereafter be placed, in supporting the
'" honor and interest of our beloved Queen and
'" country. God save the Queen!"
'His Highness appeared much gratified with the
'sentiments of the gallant Colonel, and having bowed,
'retired with General Pakenham and Sir Charles
Ogle, and remounted his charger. The sides of the
'square which were wheeled up then wheeled back,
'and the regiment formed a line. The new colours
'were now "trooped," followed by the guard in charge,
'the band playing "The Grenadiers," slow march.

1846 'On arriving at the left of the line, the colours were
'carried, and the officers marched up in the front of
'the line, one rank of the guard marching between the
'ranks of the line, and the other rank in rear of the
'rear rank. On arriving at the place where the old
'colours were stationed, the new colours took up their
'place, whilst the old ones were paraded up the re-
'maining portion of the line, the " trooping" still pro-
'ceeding, and were then delivered over to the escort
'on the right of the line; their military existence, as
'standards of the regiment, then ceasing.

'The ceremony having terminated, the Prince re-
'entered the carriage of General Pakenham, and, ac-
'companied by Admiral Sir Charles Ogle, Bart., and
'escorted by General Pakenham and staff, returned
'to the Dockyard, whence he embarked for Osborne-
'house, under salutes from the ships in harbour, the
'Platform Battery, and the Contest, Columbine, and
'Sardinian corvette at Spithead. A magnificent en-
'tertainment was given in honor of the event in the
'evening, by the officers of the THIRTEENTH, at the
'King's rooms, Southsea-beach.'

On the 3rd November, 1846, Lieut.-Colonel Squire
retired from the service, and Lieut.-Colonel A. A. T.
Cunynghame succeeded to the command of the regiment; in the following month he exchanged with
Captain and Lieut.-Colonel Charles Stuart, of the Grenadier Guards.

1847 The regiment proceeded from Portsmouth to Ireland in two divisions, on the 12th and 13th January,
1847, and arrived at Dublin on the 16th of that month.
Towards the end of September it proceeded to Birr.

1848 On the 18th of April, 1848. the regiment marched
from Birr to Newry, and on the 1st of June, to which

period the Record has been continued, the head- 1848
quarters, under the command of Lieut.-Colonel Charles
Stuart, remained at Newry, two companies being
stationed at Drogheda, and four companies being
distributed at Belturbet, Carrickmacross, Dundalk,
and Monaghan.

The preceding pages show that the THIRTEENTH, or
PRINCE ALBERT'S REGIMENT OF LIGHT INFANTRY, has
gained laurels in Europe, Asia, Africa, and America.
From the period of its declaration in favour of the
Protestant interest at the Revolution, it has run a
career of glory. Leaving the army in Flanders, in
1703, after a short campaign under the renowned
Duke of Marlborough, it next formed part of the
force in the Peninsula, and highly distinguished itself
in the first defence of Gibraltar in 1704-5, a few months
after its capture from the Spaniards. While serving
in Spain, the chivalrous Earl of Peterborough formed
the greater portion of the corps into a *cavalry* regiment;—an event unprecedented in the military history
of the British army;—in which character it proved
its bravery at the disastrous battle of Almanza.

The second defence of Gibraltar in 1727, the battle-
fields of Dettingen, Fontenoy, Falkirk, Culloden,
Roucoux, and Val, all attest its valour; while in later
times the expeditions against St. Domingo, the campaign in Egypt under the immortal Abercromby, and
the capture of Martinique, added to its ancient renown.

Recent times presented the Burmese war, in which
the regiment sustained a prominent part; latterly the
campaigns in Affghanistan, the capture of the stronghold of Ghuznee; and the advance upon Cabool, testify

I

1848 the valuable services performed; but on none of these events will the eye rest with greater interest than the defence of Jellalabad: deservedly was the garrison termed "ILLUSTRIOUS" by the Governor General in his proclamation!

Gallant deeds in all parts of the globe for upwards of a hundred and sixty years, combined with excellent conduct in quarters, have obtained for the regiment the respect of the country, and Her Majesty has graciously named it after the Royal Consort, in testimony of approbation of its many and varied services.

1848.

Description of the FLAGS *captured from the Affghans by the Thirteenth Light Infantry in the Action at Jellalabad, on the 7th April,* 1842.

The Scarlet Standard is of fine *cloth,* and is in tolerable preservation; it has a green border, with a crimson and yellow fringe; on the join, about the centre, a patch of light blue cloth is introduced, on which are neatly sewn some characters in yellow cloth, which probably form an extract from the Koran, the Affghans being known to attach great faith in such inscriptions, which are supposed to ensure victory. The flag is triangular in shape, and swallow-tailed; two of the sides are about eight and nine feet in length, the shortest side being about four feet. The staff which is the branch of a tree with the bark on, is spear-headed, but is broken at the lower extremity.

The two other Flags are but fragments; like the above they are triangular. They have pointed iron-ends to plant them in the ground. The *Crimson* flag has a green piece of cloth, with red characters, sewn in. The *Blue* flag is a sort of coarse printed cotton stuff, and has a rude shawl pattern border. There is about five feet of the flag on both the staffs, which are from eight to nine feet in length. Their appearance betokens that they have seen service, and borne the brunt of battle.

SUCCESSION OF COLONELS

OF THE

THIRTEENTH, OR, PRINCE ALBERT'S REGIMENT

OF

LIGHT INFANTRY.

THEOPHILUS EARL OF HUNTINGDON.
Appointed 20th June, 1685.

THEOPHILUS seventh EARL OF HUNTINGDON succeeded to that dignity on the decease of his father in 1655. In the reign of King Charles II. he was attached to the principles entertained by James Duke of Monmouth, who was at the head of a political party in the kingdom; but when he suspected the views of those with whom he was connected to be destructive of the constitution, he quitted their party; and in 1683 he was appointed a member of the Privy Council. He held several appointments in the reign of King James II.; was captain of the band of gentleman pensioners, now the honorable corps of gentlemen-at-arms; and on the breaking out of the rebellion of James Duke of Monmouth, in June, 1685, he exerted himself in raising men for the king's service, and was appointed colonel of one of the regiments of foot embodied on that occasion, now the THIRTEENTH Light Infantry. At the Revolution in 1688, he adhered to King James II., and being with his regiment in garrison at Plymouth, he was arrested by Colonel the Earl of Bath, Lieut.-Colonel Hastings, and other officers, who declared for the Prince of Orange. Continuing firm in his adherence to the Roman Catholic cause, he was removed from his appointments by King William, was excluded from the benefit of the Act of Indemnity passed on the 23rd of May, 1690, and upon the receipt of advice of the intended descent, in favour of King

118   SUCCESSION OF COLONELS.

James, from La Hogue, in 1692, he was sent a prisoner to the Tower of London; but he was not long detained in confinement. The Earl of Huntingdon was one of the peers who protested against the Act of Settlement in 1701. He died suddenly at his house in Charles-street, St. James's, on the 30th of May, 1701.

FERDINANDO HASTINGS.
Appointed — December, 1688.

FERDINANDO HASTINGS, cousin of Theophilus seventh Earl of Huntingdon, entered the army in the reign of King Charles II., and was promoted to the command of a company in the first foot guards; in 1686, he was appointed lieut.-colonel of the regiment which is now the THIRTEENTH Light Infantry. At the Revolution in 1688, he united with the Earl of Bath in bringing over the garrison of Plymouth to the interest of the Prince of Orange, and was rewarded with the colonelcy of his regiment. He served in Scotland under Major-General Hugh Mackay, against the clans under Viscount Dundee, and distinguished himself at the battle of Killicrankie on the 27th of June, 1689. He afterwards proceeded with his regiment to Ireland, and served at the battle of the Boyne, and at the reduction of Cork and Kinsale, in 1690: he evinced ability and personal bravery in several detached services in 1691, and served in the expedition, under the Duke of Leinster, in 1692. He was afterwards found guilty of extortion in his regiment, and was cashiered on the 4th of March, 1695.

SIR JOHN JACOB, BART.
Appointed 13*th March,* 1689.

SIR JOHN JACOB, Bart., of Bromley, in the county of Middlesex, entered the army in the summer of 1685, and was many years an officer in the regiment which is now the THIRTEENTH Light Infantry, in which corps he rose to the rank of lieut.-colonel. He evinced great courage, and received a severe wound at the battle of Killicrankie, in June, 1689, where Viscount Dundee was killed; also behaved with signal gallantry, under the eye of his sovereign, at the battle of the Boyne in 1690; and served under the Earl of Marlborough at the capture of Cork and Kinsale. King William highly approved of his conduct, and promoted him to the colonelcy of his regiment in 1695. Being afterwards desirous of retiring from the service, he obtained permission to sell his regiment to his brother-in-law, James Earl of Barrymore, for fourteen hundred guineas. He died in 1739.

JAMES EARL OF BARRYMORE.
Appointed 15th March, 1702.

JAMES, fourth EARL OF BARRYMORE, embraced the interests of the Prince of Orange at the Revolution in 1688, and was nominated lieut.-colonel in the army on the 31st of December, 1688. He subsequently held the commission of captain in the seventeenth foot, and purchased the colonelcy of the THIRTEENTH regiment in March, 1702. He was promoted to the rank of brigadier-general in 1706, and to that of major-general in 1708. He served in Portugal in the war of the Spanish succession, and led his regiment to the charge, at the battle of the Caya, on the 7th of May, 1709, with great gallantry, overthrowing all opposition, and recapturing the Portuguese guns; but not being supported by the Portuguese horse of the left wing, his regiment became insulated, and he was taken prisoner. In 1710 he was promoted to the rank of lieut.-general; and in 1713 he was sworn a member of the Privy Council. He was elected a member of the British Parliament for the Borough of Stockbridge in 1713, and afterwards for Wigan in Lancashire. He retired from his regiment in 1715. His decease occurred on the 5th of January, 1747, at Castlelyons, where a magnificent marble monument was erected to his memory.

STANHOPE COTTON.
Appointed 8th July, 1715.

THIS officer served with reputation in the wars of Queen Anne, as captain, major, and lieut.-colonel of foot; he was several years in Bowles's regiment, which was disbanded at the peace of Utrecht; and he was rewarded with the rank of colonel, and the appointment of lieut.-governor of Gibraltar. In 1715 he obtained the colonelcy of the THIRTEENTH foot, then in garrison at Gibraltar, and under his care that regiment was celebrated for its efficiency and orderly conduct. He died on the 7th of December, 1725.

Lord Mark Kerr.

Appointed 25th December, 1725.

LORD MARK KERR, fourth son of Robert fourth Earl of Lothian, entered the army on the 1st of January, 1694, and served under King William III. in Flanders. On the 1st of January, 1706, he was promoted to the colonelcy of a newly-raised regiment of foot, with which he served in the expedition under the Earl of Rivers in the same year, and when the projected descent on the coast of France was abandoned, he proceeded to Portugal, and afterwards to Spain. He commanded his regiment at the battle of Almanza, on the 25th of April, 1707, which was formed between two brigades of Portuguese cavalry which quitted the field. His regiment was engaged with very superior numbers: it behaved with great gallantry, but it was literally cut to pieces; his lordship was wounded in the arm, his lieut.-colonel and major were both killed, and his regiment lost twenty-three officers killed, wounded, and prisoners. In 1711 he was promoted to the rank of brigadier-general, and in 1712 he was nominated colonel of the twenty-ninth regiment. He commanded a brigade of infantry in the expedition to Spain, under Lord (aferwards Viscount) Cobham, in 1719, and served at the capture of Vigo. In 1725 he obtained the colonelcy of the THIRTEENTH foot,—was promoted to the rank of major-general in 1727,—removed to the eleventh dragoons in 1732, and advanced to the rank of lieut.-general in 1735. In 1740 he was appointed governor of the island of Guernsey; in 1743 he obtained the rank of general, and in 1745 he was constituted governor of Edinburgh Castle; in 1751 he was placed on the staff of Ireland. It is recorded in the Peerage of Scotland that—' He was a man of marked and decided character; with
' the strictest notions of honour and good-breeding, he re-
' tained, perhaps, too punctilious an observance of etiquette,
' as it gave him an air of frivolity. He was soldier-like in his
' appearance; formal in his deportment; whimsical, even
' finical, in his dress; but he commanded respect wherever
' he went, for none dared to laugh at his singularities. Man-
' ners, which in foreign courts, where they had been acquired,
' would have passed unobserved, were considered as fantastic
' in his own country, and were apt to lead his impatient spirit

'into rencontres too often fatal to his antagonists. Naturally
'of a good temper, his frequent appeals to the sword on
'trivial occasions drew on him the imputation of being a
'quarrelsome man; but he was inoffensive unless provoked;
'and never meddled with any one, but such as choose to
'meddle with him.' He died on the 2nd of February,
1752.

JOHN MIDDLETON.
Appointed 29th May, 1732.

JOHN MIDDLETON obtained a commission in the army in the reign of King William III., and was promoted to the rank of captain in 1706; he served in Spain in the war of the Spanish succession, and also on board the fleet, where his company was employed as Marines. He was many years an officer in the twenty-fifth foot, in which corps he rose to the rank of lieut.-colonel, and he was promoted to the rank of colonel in 1711. He commanded the twenty-fifth regiment in Scotland, under the Duke of Argyle, during the rebellion of the Earl of Mar; and in 1721 he was rewarded with the colonelcy of that corps, which he commanded until 1732, when he was removed to the THIRTEENTH foot. He was promoted to the rank of brigadier-general in 1735. His decease occurred on the 4th of May, 1739, at which period he was member of Parliament for Aberdeen.

HENRY PULTENEY.
Appointed 5th July, 1739.

HENRY PULTENEY was appointed ensign in a regiment of foot on the 10th of January, 1703, and he served in Queen Anne's wars, under the celebrated John Duke of Marlborough. He was several years in the first foot guards, and was promoted, in July, 1715, to the command of the grenadier company in the second foot guards, with the rank of lieut.-colonel. In 1733 he was promoted to the commission of second major, with the rank of colonel, and in 1734 to that of first major in the second foot guards, from which he was removed, in 1739, to the colonelcy of the THIRTEENTH regiment; at the same time he was appointed governor of Hull. He was promoted to the rank of brigadier-general in 1742, and accompanied the army to Flanders under the Earl of Stair. In 1743 he was advanced to the rank of major-general; in 1747 to that of lieut.-general, and in 1765 to that of general. On the elevation of his brother to the dignity of Earl of Bath, he was distinguished by the style of Honorable; and upon his brother's decease, without issue in 1764, he succeeded to his lordship's immense estates. He afterwards resigned his commissions. He died 26th of October, 1767.

His Royal Highness
William Henry Duke of Gloucester,
K.G., &c. &c. &c.
Appointed 25th June, 1766.

WILLIAM HENRY, third son of Frederick Prince of Wales, (who died 20th of March, 1751) was elected a Knight of the most noble order of the Garter, in 1762; and a few days before he was of full age, viz., on the 17th November, 1764, his brother, King George III., conferred on him the dignity of DUKE OF GLOUCESTER AND EDINBURGH, and Earl of Connaught; in December following he took his seat in the Privy Council. In 1766 His Royal Highness was appointed colonel of the THIRTEENTH regiment; and on the decease of his brother, Edward, Duke of York, in the autumn of 1767, he had a grant from the King of Cranburne-chase lodge, Windsor Forest. In December of the same year he was promoted to the rank of major-general, and appointed colonel of the third foot guards; and in April, 1770, he was advanced to the rank of lieut.-general, and nominated to the colonelcy of the first regiment of foot guards. He was promoted to the rank of general in 1772, and to that of field marshal in 1793. His Royal Highness was distinguished as a polite scholar and an accomplished gentleman, engaging in his manners, respectful to his sovereign, affable to his acquaintance, and generous and condescending to his inferiors; a liberal supporter of every institution calculated to promote the interests of society, accompanied by a modest serenity of conduct which kept many instances of his generosity out of public view; and a meekness of disposition pervaded every feature of his character, which insured for him the love of all ranks of society. He died on the 25th of August, 1805.

THE HONORABLE JAMES MURRAY.

Appointed 16th December, 1767.

THE HONORABLE JAMES MURRAY, son of the Duke of Athol, served several years in the fifteenth foot, of which regiment he was appointed lieut.-colonel on the 15th of January, 1751. He served with his regiment in North America, in the early part of the seven years' war, had the local rank of colonel in that country on the 7th of January, 1758, and was appointed colonel-commandant in the sixtieth, Royal American regiment, on the 24th of October, 1759. He also served in Germany, under Prince Ferdinand of Brunswick, and was wounded in the breast with a musket ball, which could not be extracted, and he was never afterwards able to sleep in a recumbent posture. He was promoted to the rank of major-general in 1762, appointed colonel of the THIRTEENTH regiment in 1767, in succession to His Royal Highness the Duke of Gloucester, advanced to the rank of lieut.-general in 1772, to that of general in 1783, and removed to the twenty-first, or Royal North British Fusiliers, in 1789. He also held the appointment of governor of Hull. He died in 1794, and was buried in Westminster Abbey.

GEORGE AINSLIE.

Appointed 5th June, 1789.

THIS officer was appointed in 1755, sub-lieutenant in the second, or Scots, troop of horse grenadier guards, of which the celebrated General Eliott, afterwards Lord Heathfield, Baron Gibraltar, was lieut.-colonel; and when Colonel Eliott raised his famed regiment of "Light Horse," now the fifteenth, or King's Hussars, lieutenant Ainslie was appointed captain of the first troop in that regiment. He proceeded with the fifteenth light dragoons to Germany, in 1760, and distinguished himself in the memorable action at Emsdorf, where his regiment acquired great honour. He was also present at numerous other actions, where "Eliott's Light Horse" availed themselves of every opportunity to acquire additional laurels; and on the 29th of March, 1762, he was promoted to the majority of the regiment. At the engagement near Homburg, on the 1st of July, 1762, he highly distinguished himself, and was commended in the public despatch of Prince Ferdinand of Brunswick. In the action near Friedberg, on the 30th of August following, he was attacked by three French hussars, and received a dangerous wound in the head. He was promoted to the lieut.-colonelcy of the fifteenth light dragoons in 1770, to the rank of colonel in the army in 1779, and to that of major-general in 1782: in 1789 King George III. rewarded him with the colonelcy of the THIRTEENTH foot, His Majesty having frequently witnessed, and expressed his high approbation of, the condition of the fifteenth light dragoons under colonel Ainslie's command. He was afterwards appointed lieut.-governor of Scilly Island, was promoted to the rank of lieut.-general in 1796, and to that of general in 1801. He died in 1804.

ALEXANDER CAMPBELL.

Appointed 11th July, 1804.

ON the 21st of April, 1769, Alexander Campbell was appointed ensign in the forty-second, Royal Highland regiment, then in Ireland, and in December,1770, he was promoted to a lieutenancy in the second battalion of the Royals, which he joined at the island of Minorca; in September, 1772, he was advanced to captain of a company in the fiftieth, from which he exchanged to the sixty-second regiment in November following. He embarked for Canada with the sixty-second on the breaking out of the American war, and served the campaign of 1776, under General Carleton, afterwards Lord Dorchester. In 1777, he served under Lieut.-General Burgoyne, in the desperate attempt to advance from Canada, through the country, in a state of rebellion, to Albany, shared in the toils and fighting of that enterprise, and was included in the convention at Saratoga. On the 26th of December, 1777, he was promoted to major of the seventy-fourth regiment, and proceeding to New York, he was appointed to act as major of the first battalion of light infantry, with which he served two campaigns, and at the termination of the war he commanded at Penobscot. On the 31st of December, 1782, he was promoted to the lieut.-colonelcy of the sixty-second foot, with which regiment he served in Scotland and Ireland until June, 1789, when he exchanged to captain and lieut.-colonel in the third foot guards. He served the campaign of 1793, and part of that of 1794, in Flanders, under His Royal Highness the Duke of York; he had, in the meantime, been promoted to the rank of colonel (12th October, 1793), and commissioned to raise the 116th regiment of foot, and he withdrew from Flanders. He subsequently commanded a brigade in the forces under Lieut.-General the Earl of Moira, and was promoted to the rank of major-general, on the 26th of February, 1795. In 1796 he served under Lieut.-General Sir Ralph Abercromby, in the West Indies, and was appointed colonel of the seventh West India regiment, in November of that year. He served on the staff at Newcastle in 1797; in Ireland in 1798; and afterwards in Scotland. In 1802 his regiment was disbanded; he was promoted to the rank of lieut.-general in April of that year, and was placed on the staff of Ireland, and subsequently on that of Scotland, where he served five years. In 1804 he was appointed colonel of the THIRTEENTH regiment; in 1812 he was promoted to the rank of general, and was removed to the thirty-second regiment in 1813. He died 24th of February, 1832.

EDWARD MORRISON.

Appointed 15th February, 1813.

THIS officer entered the army as an ensign in the Coldstream Guards, on the 20th January, 1777; was shortly after employed as Assistant Quartermaster-General; and on the 15th September, 1780, succeeded to a lieutenancy with the rank of captain: from November 1781, to June, 1783, he served as aide-de-camp to the commander-in-chief in the West Indies. He was promoted to a company, with the rank of lieut.-colonel on 13th January, 1790, and in 1793, was appointed Deputy Quartermaster-General; but obtained permission to join the first battalion of the Coldstream Guards in Flanders, in 1794. He was appointed Governor of Chester on 2nd November, 1796. On the 26th February, 1795, he received the brevet rank of colonel; and on the 19th November, 1800, was appointed colonel of the Leicester fencibles, and on 1st January, 1805, of a battalion in the sixtieth regiment. He was advanced to the rank of major-general on the

1st January, 1798, and in April following was appointed to the Staff in Ireland, where he commanded the Limerick District during the rebellion. He was removed to the Staff in England in July, 1803, and on the 1st January, 1805, was advanced to the rank of lieut.-general; in May, 1809, was appointed lieut.-general and commander of the forces at Jamaica; and was promoted to the rank of general, on the 4th June, 1814. On the 15th February of the previous year, His Majesty King George III. conferred on him the colonelcy of the THIRTEENTH light infantry, which he held to the period of his decease, which occurred on the 3rd December, 1843.

SIR ROBERT HENRY SALE, G.C.B.
Appointed 15th December, 1843.

AT the early age of fourteen this officer had the honour of carrying his Sovereign's colours as an ensign in the thirty-sixth regiment, to which he was gazetted on the 19th January, 1795: he was promoted to a lieutenancy on the 12th April, 1797, and on the 8th January following exchanged into the twelfth foot, with which regiment he served at the battle of Mallavelly gained by Lieut.-general (afterwards Lord) Harris on the 27th March, 1799. In less than two months occurred the siege of Seringapatam, where Lieutenant Sale's services were rewarded by a medal. He served throughout the campaign of 1801, in the Wynaud country, and on the 23rd March, 1806, obtained his company. Captain Sale took part in the storming of the Travancore lines in 1809; and was at the capture of the Mauritius in 1810. On the 30th December, 1813, he was promoted to the rank of Major, and the second battalion of the twelfth being reduced in January, 1818, Major Sale was placed on the half-pay. On the 28th June, 1821, he exchanged to the THIRTEENTH light infantry, with which he proceeded to India, joined the expedition under Major-General Sir Archibald Campbell, and served throughout the Burmese war, being present at the capture of Rangoon and the storming of the stockades near Kemmendine, on both occasions displaying such heroism, that he received the thanks of the commanding officer on the field of battle, and particular notice in the general orders. He also stormed the seven stockades near Kumaroot and Pagoda Point: on the 1st December, of the same year (1824) he stormed the enemy's lines, and on the 5th of that month led a body of 1600 men in the engagement which resulted in the utter defeat of the foe, who was driven from all his positions. On the 8th December, he commanded in the attack on the rear of the enemy's lines opposite the Great Pagoda at Rangoon; and on the 15th, stormed the intrenchments at Kokien, where he was severely wounded in the head. In the following year, he commanded a brigade at the reduction of Bassein, and subsequent operations from 10th February to 2nd May, 1825. On the 2nd June, 1825, he attained the rank of lieut.-colonel; on the 1st December, he commanded the first brigade and repulsed the Shaans and Burmese at Prome, and the next day stormed the lines and heights near Prome. He was again severely wounded at the storming of Melloon on the 19th January, 1826. These services were honored with the riband of a companion of the order of the Bath. He became colonel by brevet on the 28th June, 1838, and in the following October, was appointed to the command of the first Bengal brigade of the army of the Indus, which formed the advance throughout the campaign in Affghanistan: he commanded the detachment of 2500 men sent to Girishk in May, 1839, and on the 23rd July, headed the storming party which captured the fortress of Ghuznee, deemed by the Affghans impregnable. A sabre-wound in the chin and contusions on the chest and shoulder from musket-shots were the results of this formidable conflict; but not the only results, for his services were acknowledged by Lord Keane, and Her Majesty conferred upon him the star of a Knight Commander of the Bath, and his name was enrolled in the list of Eastern Knights constituting the order of the Dooranee Empire, which had been founded by Shah-Shoojah. In September, 1840, the forces sent to subdue the Kohistan country were entrusted to his command; and after storming the towns and fort of Tootumdurra, Julgar, Babookooshghur, Kardurrah, and Purwan, he compelled Dost Mahomed to surrender to the authorites at Cabool. In forcing the Khoord Cabool Pass on the 12th October, 1841, he was shot through the leg. His gallant defence of Jellalabad,—his daring sorties, and final defeat of the besieging army under Akbar Khan, for which services he received the thanks of Parliament, and was nominated a Knight Grand Cross of the Most Honorable Military Order of the Bath, are detailed in the Regimental Record, and completely identify Sir Robert Sale's name with the THIRTEENTH light infantry, the connexion being rendered more intimate by Her Majesty, who conferred on him the colonelcy of the regiment in December, 1843, on the decease of General Edward Morrison. On the 29th March, 1844, he was appointed by Her Majesty, Quartermaster-General to the Queen's troops serving in the East Indies. Advancing with the army to repel the Sikh invasion, Sir Robert Sale had his left thigh so dreadfully shattered by a grapeshot at the battle of Moodkee on the 18th December, 1845, that he did not long survive the wound, but, after a distinguished career, fell like Wolfe, Sir John Moore, and other heroes, in the hour of victory.

LIEUT.-GENERAL SIR WILLIAM MAYNARD GOMM, K.C.B.

Appointed 10*th March*, 1846.

www.ingramcontent.com/pod-product-compliance
Lightning Source LLC
Chambersburg PA
CBHW041927090426
42743CB00021B/3464